SLOW COOK ALL DAY

SLOW COOK ALL DAY

THE ULTIMATE COOKBOOK OF HANDS-OFF SLOW COOKER RECIPES

PAULA JONES

PHOTOGRAPHY BY IAIN BAGWELL

ROCKRIDGE
PRESS

For general information on our other products and services or to obtain technical support, please contact our Customer Care Department within the United States at (866) 744-2665, or outside the United States at (510) 253-0500.

Rockridge Press publishes its books in a variety of electronic and print formats. Some content that appears in print may not be available in electronic books, and vice versa.

Interior and Cover Designer: Michael Cook
Art Producer: Hannah Dickerson
Editor: Van Van Cleave
Production Editor: Ruth Sakata Corley

Photography © 2020 Iain Bagwell; food styling by Loren Wood

Author photo courtesy of Laura Oliver of Ransom Photography

ISBN: Print 978-1-64739-035-8 | eBook 978-1-64739-036-5

R0

For everyone trying their best to get a meal
on the table every night, I see you.
I know it's not always easy.
My hope is you'll find new family favorites
in this book to help you do just that
while saving precious time.

CONTENTS

INTRODUCTION

Welcome to one-pot-wonder slow cooking. The one-pot wonder I'm referring to is a slow cooker, otherwise known as that oval or round countertop appliance you may have received as a graduation, wedding, or housewarming gift. Go ahead, grab it and dust it off because I'm going to help you put that baby to good use.

How? With 100 easy, delicious, and nutritionally balanced recipes for your slow cooker that all take eight hours or more to cook. In this book, you'll find everything from comforting soups, stews, and chilis to plant-based vegetarian and vegan meals. And I didn't forget my meat-loving friends. Carnivores can enjoy meaty marvels with recipes that feature chicken, turkey, beef, pork, lamb, and veal. There's even a staples chapter where you can learn to make your own stocks and sauces. I also share tips throughout to help you maximize your slow cooker's potential.

All the recipes in this book are perfect for anyone and everyone who wants to eat home-cooked meals made with minimal effort. These are not the slow cooker recipes of yore. They're fun, flavorful, and fast to prep—slow cooker recipes for our busy lifestyles.

Cooking is my love language, and one of my greatest joys is sharing food with the people I love. I've been cooking for as long as I can remember, certainly since I was tall enough to stand on a chair in the kitchen and stir. I love to cook all types of foods, but especially meals that are quick to prep and simple to cook, so it's no surprise I love slow cooking. My hope is that after trying my recipes, you will too.

Why do I love cooking with a slow cooker? It's convenient and budget-friendly. We're all super busy these days. Between work, family obligations, and attempting to have a social life, we're running ourselves thin, including me. Using a slow cooker not only helps me save time (hello, set it and forget it), it also helps me save money. How? Because I don't have to stop last minute to figure out what to pick up for dinner and overspend in the process. If I can do this, so can you. We got this!

I would love to invite you to my table to share a meal but, sadly, that isn't possible. Instead, my hope is you'll enjoy making these recipes and sharing them with your own friends and family. Feel free to share what you make with me virtually on social media using #bellalimento.

Now, let's go explore a slew of slow cooking possibilities!

CHAPTER ONE

COOKING SLOW WHEN YOU'RE ON THE GO

You're busy. I'm busy. Everyone's busy these days, and sometimes the thought of preparing dinner is daunting. But it doesn't have to be. With just a little help from you before you head out the door to start your day, your superstar slow cooker can do most of the hard work. And that means you come home to delicious home-cooked meals, no personal chef required.

Not sure how to make the most of this wonder appliance? I'm here to help. In this book, you'll learn everything you need to know about slow cooking, including 100 simple recipes, pro tips for cooking hearty meals, strategies for making prep easy, and helpful logistics such as storage information to maximize leftovers. So sit back, relax, and let this book be your guide to slow cooker magic.

SAVOR YOUR TIME

Did you know, what we know as today's slow cooker has been around since the 1970s? It's 50-ish years old and still fabulous. The inspiration for the slow cooker was a simmer crock from the 1940s that was used solely to simmer beans. It was called the Naxon Beanery All-Purpose Cooker and owned by—you guessed it—Naxon. A rival company purchased Naxon in the 1970s, acquiring their patent and design. They reimagined and tweaked the crock so it could cook an entire family meal, not just beans, which made it a much more desirable kitchen appliance. The new owner then followed up by trademarking the name Crock-Pot. The Crock-Pot brand has since been acquired by Sunbeam and now is just one of many slow cooker brands on the market.

Though slow cookers are often associated with your grandma's casseroles, that's not the case anymore. Slow cookers are making a major comeback, and with good reason. A slow cooker is a modern-day kitchen hero and one of the most convenient small appliances you can own. It simplifies home cooking and caters to our often very busy lifestyles. Any small appliance that can make life easier certainly earns its place on my precious countertop real estate. I hope you're nodding in agreement.

But the very best part about a slow cooker? It does the cooking for you so you can go about your day. However, if you work a 9-to-5 job, that ability is only useful if the recipe takes eight or more hours to cook and doesn't require you to fiddle with it at any point. Good news: I have you covered. All the recipes in this book take eight or more hours, so you can truly set it and forget it.

Not all heroes wear capes; some wear lids.

LONG-HAUL SLOW COOKING

What exactly is long-haul slow cooking? In a nutshell, it's low and slow all-day cooking. Easy peasy, load and go, fix it and forget it—all terms you'll hear throughout this book. We're in it for the long haul together. Can I get a virtual high five?

As I mentioned, all the recipes in this book cook on Low heat for eight or more hours. I always use a 6-quart slow cooker for consistency. The recipes require minimal prep, some of which can even be done the night before. Most meals are ready to be served as soon as the timer goes off, and those that do require a small amount of assembly after cooking take no more than 15 minutes, for minimal effort and maximum results. Sound good?

Slow cookers aren't just for pot roasts, although those are incredibly delicious and there is most definitely a pot roast recipe included in this book. But variety is the spice of life and so you'll find 100 recipes here.

You'll see filling and comforting slow-cooked soups, such as the classic French Onion Soup (page 22), Thai-Inspired Coconut Soup with Chicken (page 35), and an Enchilada Soup (page 21) that I am currently obsessed with, as well as chilis, including Turkey, Black Bean, and Pumpkin Chili (page 36) and a creamy White Chicken Chili (page 37). If thick, hearty stews are more your style, try Guinness Beef Stew (page 24).

Wondering about vegetarian and vegan options? I've got those covered, too. Sweet Potato Curry (page 61), Red Beans and Rice (page 59), Calabacitas (page 48), and even Rice-Stuffed Cabbage Rolls (page 53) will satisfy your plant-based cravings.

Poultry more your jam? Try Salsa Chicken with Black Beans and Corn (page 83), Chicken Tikka Masala (page 88), Chicken Marsala (page 71), or what about Turkey Meatballs (page 87), because who doesn't love a good meatball?

Of course, I couldn't leave out beef, pork, and lamb options. You'll crave the Classic Pulled Pork (page 115) all year long, and the Veal Osso Buco (page 116) will make you want to sing.

I've also included a chapter for staples such as broths, stocks, and sauces that you can use in tandem with recipes throughout the book. Don't worry, I'll teach you the difference between stock and broth and even remind you when you're cooking chicken to save the bones to make Chicken Stock (page 125). The sumptuous sauce recipes, such as Enchilada Sauce (page 129) and Meaty Spaghetti Sauce (page 131), can all be stored for use in other dishes, so you'll be able to cut down on day-of prep even more.

All you have to do now is decide which recipe to start with!

WHAT YOU WON'T SEE

Some foods are naturally suited to the slow cooker's long, slow, moist cooking times, such as large fatty cuts of meats (e.g., beef or pork roasts) that require longer cooking times to break down and become tender.

However, even heroes have their limits. Some foods should not be cooked in the slow cooker. To that end, you won't see any seafood-focused meals in this book. Seafood does not take well to long cook times, and seafood kept at warm temperatures for long periods can be unsafe to eat. Save that shrimp for quicker stovetop, grilling, or oven preparations.

You also won't see any canned cream of anything here. That's not for any safety reasons, just preference. To keep recipes nourishing and tasty, I rely mainly on fresh ingredients. However, I do include some canned items, such as tomatoes, corn, and beans, which allow you to whip up meals easily and quickly. Who has the patience to rehydrate dried beans, anyway?

KNOW YOUR SLOW COOKER

Because cooking long and slow can be a sensitive business, it's important to know the quirks of your particular slow cooker. All slow cookers are different. Some are very basic with just Low, High, and Off settings. Some have handy upgrades such as programmable timers. Some are quite fancy and can include Wi-Fi enabled features you control from your phone while you're away from home. As such, you'll want to be sure to read your slow cooker's instruction manual and always follow the manufacturer's instructions for your particular slow cooker.

For this book, I used several different slow cookers: a 6-quart programmable Cook & Carry Crock-Pot, a 6-quart Hamilton Beach slow cooker, and the slow cooker feature of a 6-quart Instant Pot. Each have different price points and options, but all have a 6-quart capacity.

GET WITH THE PROGRAM

Of the three slow cookers just mentioned, the programmable 6-quart Cook & Carry Crock-Pot slow cooker had the advantage for me. I liked that I could set the timer for eight hours, and when that time was up, the cooker automatically switched to the Keep Warm feature. I also appreciated that the cooker came with latches to secure the lid to the vessel for easy transportation. In instances where I would take a meal to a potluck, family gathering, or tailgate, this feature came in handy. For anyone who has ever tried to transport a slow cooker in a vehicle only to have it spill, you'll appreciate the latch feature. It delivers on the Cook & Carry concept.

If your slow cooker doesn't have a programmable feature, do not fear! You can use a programmable digital plug-in switch called a socket timer. It can be plugged into your slow cooker, giving you the ability to set a timer, just as you would use for setting indoor lights to switch on.

SIZE MATTERS

The size of the vessel directly affects cooking times. It's important to not over-crowd your slow cooker. The vessel should not be filled more than two-thirds full. If the recipe is written for a 6-quart slow cooker, make sure you use a 6-quart slow cooker.

WATCH THE HEAT

Just like an oven or stove, every slow cooker model seems to cook food a bit differently. The best way to determine whether your appliance tends to run hotter or colder (and thus requires a bit more or a bit less cooking time) is by doing some test runs.

SET AND FORGET LIKE A PRO

One of my mottos in all things, including cooking, is to work smarter, not harder. In keeping with that motto, here are a few tips and tricks to help you set and forget your slow cooker meals like a pro.

IT'S ALL ABOUT THE TIMING. If you don't have a programmable slow cooker, I strongly encourage you to look into purchasing a programmable timer. This will ensure you have the most control over cook times, even though you may not be at home. These timers even come in handy if you're a stay-at-home parent and/or if you work from home. The day can get away from you, but with a timer, your meal doesn't have to.

MAKE FOOD BEST SUITED TO LONG COOK TIMES. As noted earlier, certain foods are more suited to longer cook times. I provide more detail about this in "Slow Cooker Standouts" (see page 7). Additionally, for even cooking, cut food as uniformly as possible and then layer items in the cooker in order of how long they take to cook. Potatoes, carrots, etc., on the bottom and meat on top.

THINK ABOUT THICKENER. Using certain ingredients may help your sauce stand up to moist conditions. Cornstarch and flour are both thickening agents you most likely have in your pantry.

BE MINDFUL OF SPACE. The more empty space you have in the slow cooker, the faster the food will cook. Do not fill your cooker more than two-thirds full, though.

SAVE FROZEN FOOD FOR THE FREEZER. Make sure items are properly thawed in advance of cooking. This ensures your slow cooker operates at the correct temperature, keeping your food safe to eat.

KEEP A LID ON IT. If you are at home, resist the urge to pull off the lid and peek. If you do, as with opening an oven door, you'll let out the heat and the cooker will take additional time to come back to temperature. Be patient.

SLOW COOKER STANDOUTS

Some foods are naturally suited to the slow cooker's long, slow, moist cooking times. These are the ingredients you'll see used most often in this cookbook.

Beans. Beans are rich in protein and a great budget-friendly addition to recipes. I mainly use black beans and kidney beans throughout the book.

Broth and stock. We have recipes for homemade versions of both broth and stock in this book, but you may substitute canned, if you wish. If you do, I recommend using a low-sodium option so you control the amount of salt in your food.

Canned tomatoes. Tomato sauce, tomato paste, and diced tomatoes are pantry staples in most homes and are used in the recipes in this book frequently. When tomatoes aren't in season, good quality canned tomatoes are a great substitute. Look for tomatoes picked and canned at peak ripeness.

Fatty cuts of meat. Larger cuts of meat, such as beef or pork roasts, are well suited to the slow cooker's method of cooking.

Root vegetables. Carrots, potatoes, sweet potatoes, parsnips, celery root, and turnips contain lots of fiber and many vitamins and minerals. They cook to tender perfection in the slow cooker.

Spices. Spices bring depth and flavor to foods. Not to worry, though; there are no exotic spices to hunt down. All spices in these recipes can be easily sourced, and you may even have most of them in your pantry already.

QUICK AND EASY PREP

Your future self will thank you for putting in a little work in advance of cooking the meal. Especially if you're not a morning person (like me).

MVP PREP TOOLS

CHEF'S KNIFE: A good sharp knife is the one of the best investments you can make in your kitchen. Choose a knife that feels comfortable and secure in your hand. Take into consideration the knife's weight, shape, and size.

CUTTING BOARD: You'll need a wooden cutting board as well as flexible cutting mats for cutting, dicing, slicing, and chopping. Wood cutting boards are durable and are great for heavy-duty usage. The benefit of using flexible cutting mats is that they're dishwasher safe and you're able to funnel ingredients easily and directly into the pan or slow cooker insert.

MANDOLINE: This cutting tool helps you slice ingredients quickly and evenly. Because a mandoline blade is extremely sharp, always use the safety guard. For slicing onions alone, a small mandoline is worth the price of admission.

NONSTICK COOKING SPRAY: This helps foods easily release from the stoneware slow cooker insert. I prefer to use this method rather than using slow cooker liners.

SLOW COOKER LINERS (OPTIONAL): These are, essentially, plastic bags used to line your slow cooker for fast and easy cleanup. They can be found in most grocery stores in the aisle with zip-top bags, aluminum foil, and plastic wrap.

OPTIONAL FLAVOR BOOST

When possible, I recommend browning meats during your prep work, before slow cooking, for a flavor boost. A little extra time up front yields a deeper flavor in the end.

PREP AHEAD STRATEGIES

There are many strategies to ensure your morning prep sessions go as smoothly as possible. Consider these tips:

Start with a clean slate. Make sure you clean your work surface and slow cooker before you begin. If you have a dishwasher, make sure it's empty. Stacking dishes in the sink to deal with after dinner only means a headache later.

Read the entire recipe first. Don't skim it. You wouldn't want to accidentally use garlic salt when the recipe calls for garlic powder and have your dish turn out too salty.

Check your ingredients. Before you start cooking, check your refrigerator and pantry to make sure you have all the ingredients needed for the recipe.

Use store-bought shortcuts. Prepared broths, stocks, sauces, and vegetables can all work in a pinch.

Prep materials and ingredients the night before. Set out any nonperishable items, such as spices and canned goods, the night before, along with the measuring cups and spoons you'll need, a can opener, a rimmed baking sheet, cutting mats, etc. Whenever possible, peel, chop, slice, dice, and properly store any items the recipe calls for in advance. Last but never least, make sure your meat is completely thawed.

ENSURING FLAVOR SUCCESS

A common pitfall of long-cooking recipes is that they lose flavor, but not to fear; there are easy ways to ensure this doesn't happen.

SPICE IS NICE. Salt, pepper, and additional herbs and spices are your friends. Keep them close and you'll start and end each dish with a bang.

TASTE BEFORE SERVING. Salt it like you mean it and be sure to taste everything before serving. Remember, it's easier to add more than it is to take away.

USE BRIGHT, FRESH FLAVORS AT THE END. Fresh herbs not only add a flavor punch, they also add a fun pop of color. Chopped fresh parsley, cilantro, basil, and thyme are a few of my favorites. A squeeze of fresh lemon or lime juice can quickly add zip and zest. A drizzle of good quality olive oil is also always a winner.

SPICE IT UP

A few superstar spices go a long way when cooking. Following is a list of this book's commonly used, and easily sourced, spices. Keep in mind that dried herbs are, typically, more potent than fresh herbs, so use one-third to half as much dried as you would fresh. If you're looking for even more variety in herbs and spices, check the international aisle of your grocery store.

Chili powder: This is the pulverized dried fruit of chile peppers, plus additional spices that vary based on the brand you purchase. Chili powder's flavor really blooms during long cooking processes and shines in many of the recipes in this book.

Cumin: This is the dried seed of the herb Cuminum, a member of the parsley family. Cumin is warm and earthy in taste and complements other spices nicely.

Dried basil: This is the dried form of fresh basil. It tastes mild and slightly sweet.

Dried oregano: This is a dried form of fresh oregano and brings a peppery bite to dishes.

Garlic powder: This is dehydrated ground garlic. Many recipes in this book opt for garlic powder instead of whole garlic for convenience and ease of mixing.

Kosher salt and black pepper: I use kosher salt in all the recipes in this book, as well as freshly ground black pepper. You can find pre-filled small pepper mills in most grocery stores these days, or you can purchase peppercorns to use in your peppermill.

Onion powder: This is dehydrated ground onion. Many recipes in this book opt for onion powder instead of fresh onion, for convenience and ease of mixing.

FOOD SAFETY AND STORAGE

Food safety and storage are always extremely important, but especially when food is going to be cooked for long periods. The following general recommended guidelines are from the United States Department of Agriculture (USDA). Please visit the USDA's website for more specific information.

FOOD SAFETY

Safety is important in everything in life and food safety is no exception. Here are some tips to keep you on track.

START CLEAN. As when doing any cooking, you'll want to use clean equipment. Make sure your slow cooker, all your utensils, and your work area are completely clean before you begin prepping and cooking.

KEEP COOL. Keep perishable foods in the refrigerator until it is time to add them to the slow cooker insert. Bacteria multiply rapidly when food is left at room temperature and that puts everyone at risk of illness.

TAKE THE CHILL OFF. Always defrost any meat or poultry before you put it in the slow cooker. Why? When you put frozen meat or poultry in a slow cooker, it can spend too much time thawing, instead of cooking, which allows bacteria to multiply, and that can make you sick. Using fully thawed foods ensures your meal cooks evenly and completely for best results.

DON'T "FILL 'ER UP." Make sure your slow cooker is no more than half to two-thirds full to ensure foods cook through. No overfilling!

FREEZING AND REFRIGERATING

If you're lucky enough to have leftovers, and I hope you are because that makes lunch the following day a no-brainer, it's good to know how to properly refrigerate or freeze them.

COOL DOWN. Refrigerate leftovers within two hours of finishing cooking so foods remain out of the temperature danger zone and bacteria don't form.

PUT A LID ON IT. Store your food in shallow sealable containers to keep it safe from outside contaminants.

TYPE OF FOOD	REFRIGERATOR STORAGE	FREEZER STORAGE
Chicken, turkey, and other poultry	3 to 4 days	4 months
Soups and stews	4 to 5 days	2 to 3 months
Beef, lamb, pork, and veal	3 to 4 days	2 to 3 months
Stocks	3 to 5 days	3 months

THAWING AND REHEATING

Now that you've properly stored your leftovers, here's how to thaw and reheat them properly so you can safely and deliciously enjoy them.

PLAN AHEAD. It's best to plan ahead so you can thaw your food slowly and safely in the refrigerator. Small items may defrost overnight, but most foods require a day or two to thaw completely. A good rule of thumb is one day of thawing for each five pounds of weight.

THE HEAT IS ON. Reheating leftovers directly in a slow cooker is **not** recommended. Cooked food should be reheated on the stovetop, in the microwave, or in your oven until it reaches 165°F. Then, if you wish, you can transfer the hot food to a preheated slow cooker to keep it warm for serving.

LET'S GET COOKING

Before you rev up that slow cooker, here are a few final reminders of what treasures lie in store for you. Please also remember that all 100 recipes in this book were tested in and are recommended for a 6-quart slow cooker on Low heat for eight hours. Now on to all those tasty features!

A VARIETY OF FLAVORS. There are so many flavor profiles included in this book, inspired by the delicious cuisines of different cultures across the world. With so many options, I predict there are at least a few recipes that will become new family favorites.

NUTRITIONALLY BALANCED MEALS THAT TAKE 8+ HOURS TO COOK. These recipes are truly "set and forget," so you can come home to perfect weeknight meals every time.

RECIPES WITH MINIMAL PREP REQUIRED. To make your life easier, the recipes take no longer than 15 minutes to prep, and very few recipes require any precooking.

OPTIONAL HOMEMADE STAPLES. A chapter of homemade broths, stocks, and sauces is available if you prefer to make your own. You can easily freeze them to have on hand when you need them.

INFORMATIVE DIETARY LABELS. When applicable, the recipes feature dietary labels to help you follow whichever diet you prefer. Look for dairy-free, nut-free, and vegetarian/vegan labels.

TIPS TO MAKE COOKING EASIER. You'll find a variety of tips throughout the book to help you gain confidence in the kitchen, from prepping ahead to employing optional techniques for boosting flavor.

**THAI-INSPIRED COCONUT
SOUP WITH CHICKEN, 35**

SOUPS, STEWS, AND CHILIS

CHICKEN STEW

Chicken stew is not only budget friendly because you're using chicken legs, it's also incredibly versatile. Eat it as-is or serve it over rice or egg noodles to stretch your meal. Finish the stew with a handful of chopped fresh parsley to brighten it up. I always save chicken bones in a freezer bag in the freezer until I have enough to make homemade Chicken Stock (page 125) or Chicken Broth (page 124).

4 chicken legs, skin removed and discarded

3 potatoes, peeled and diced

2 carrots, cut into 2-inch pieces

1 small onion, finely chopped

2 garlic cloves, minced

1 tablespoon Italian seasoning (preferably Zoe's Spice of Life)

5 cups Chicken Stock (page 125)

1 to 2 teaspoons cornstarch

4 ounces mushrooms, sliced

Salt

Freshly ground black pepper

2 tablespoons chopped fresh parsley

Serves **8**
Prep time: **15 minutes**
Cook time: **8 hours (Low),**
plus 15 minutes (High)
DAIRY-FREE
NUT-FREE

Tip: Prepare the vegetables the night before to save time in the morning.

Per Serving (1 cup)
Calories: 282; Fat: 6g;
Protein: 29g;
Total Carbohydrates: 28g;
Fiber: 4g; Sugar: 2g;
Sodium: 213mg

1. In your slow cooker insert, stir together the chicken, potatoes, carrots, onion, garlic, Italian seasoning, and chicken stock. Cover the cooker and cook on Low heat for 8 hours.

2. Remove the chicken. Carefully remove the meat from the bones, cut up into pieces, and set aside. Save the bones for stock (see headnote).

3. In a small bowl, make a slurry by stirring together the cornstarch and a few tablespoons of the stew liquid until dissolved. Stir the slurry into the stew.

4. Return the chicken to the slow cooker insert. Add the mushrooms. Stir to combine. Cover the cooker and cook on High heat for about 15 minutes more until the sauce thickens and the mushrooms are cooked through. Taste and add salt and pepper, as needed. Spoon the stew into bowls and serve warm, topped with a sprinkle of parsley.

5. Refrigerate any leftovers in an airtight container or freeze for future use (see chart, page 12).

CLASSIC BEEF CHILI

Chili is a crowd-pleaser and with good reason: It's rich, hearty, and—you guessed it!—makes enough to feed a crowd. Serve this chili over rice, like I do, to stretch it. The rice also cuts a bit of the heat for those who like things on the milder side. Garnish with as much or as little as you like. I like shredded cheese, sour cream, Fritos, or scallions.

1 tablespoon extra-virgin olive oil

1 small onion, finely chopped

1 pound ground beef

2 tablespoons chili powder

2 teaspoons ground cumin

2 teaspoons smoked paprika

1 teaspoon kosher salt

¼ teaspoon cayenne pepper

2 (14.5-ounce) cans diced tomatoes

1 (15.5-ounce) can kidney beans, drained and rinsed

1 (15.5-ounce) can mild chili beans in chili sauce

Serves **10**
Prep time: **15 minutes**
Cook time: **8 hours (Low)**
DAIRY-FREE
NUT-FREE

Tip: Prep and sauté the onion and brown the beef the night before to save time in the morning. Cover and refrigerate until assembly.

Per Serving (1 cup)
Calories: 159; Fat: 5g;
Protein: 15g;
Total Carbohydrates: 16g;
Fiber: 4g; Sugar: 3g;
Sodium: 347mg

1. In a heavy-bottomed pan over medium heat, heat the olive oil. Add the onion and sauté until softened. Add the beef and cook, breaking the beef up with a spoon, until it is evenly browned and no longer pink. Drain and transfer to your slow cooker insert.

2. Stir in the chili powder, cumin, paprika, salt, cayenne, tomatoes with their juices, kidney beans, and chili beans. Cover the cooker and cook on Low heat for 8 hours.

3. Refrigerate any leftovers in an airtight container or freeze for future use (see chart, page 12).

CLASSIC CHICKEN NOODLE SOUP

There is just something comforting about a big bowl of homemade chicken noodle soup. It's soothing, regardless of whether you're under the weather or not. Using homemade chicken stock takes this recipe from bam to BOOM. If you do happen to use store-bought stock, choose a lower-sodium option so you control the amount of salt in your soup. This recipe makes a large batch, but leftovers hold up well and make a great next-day lunch option.

2 boneless, skinless chicken breasts

3 carrots, cut into coins

2 celery stalks, chopped

½ onion, finely chopped

2 bay leaves

1 teaspoon kosher salt, plus more for seasoning

¼ teaspoon freshly ground black pepper, plus more for seasoning

8 cups Chicken Stock (page 125)

3 cups dried egg noodles

Serves **10**
Prep time: **15 minutes**
Cook time: **8 hours (Low)**, **plus 15 minutes (High)**
DAIRY-FREE
NUT-FREE

Tips: Prepare the vegetables the night before to save time in the morning. Save the vegetable scraps (ends, peels) and use them to make Vegetable Broth (page 127).

Per Serving (1 cup)
Calories: 76; Fat: 1g;
Protein: 7g;
Total Carbohydrates: 10g;
Fiber: 1g; Sugar: 1g;
Sodium: 142mg

1. In your slow cooker insert, stir together the chicken, carrots, celery, onion, bay leaves, salt, pepper, and chicken stock. Cover the cooker and cook on Low heat for 8 hours.

2. Remove the chicken and discard the bay leaves.

3. Add the egg noodles to the slow cooker, adjust the setting to High heat, and re-cover the cooker. Cook for 10 to 15 minutes or more until the noodles are cooked through.

4. Using two forks, shred the chicken, then return it to the slow cooker. Stir to combine. Taste and add more salt or pepper, as needed.

5. Refrigerate any leftovers in an airtight container or freeze for future use (see chart, page 12).

CREAMY CHICKEN AND WILD RICE SOUP

Chances are you've had a chicken and rice casserole at some point in your life; well, this soup is a riff on that. It's hearty, thick, and delicious, thanks to the incredibly creamy wild rice. If you prefer your wild rice on the firmer side, cook it the night before and add it at the end of the recipe, cooking it just until it's warmed through.

1 boneless, skinless chicken breast

1 cup uncooked wild rice

2 celery stalks, chopped

1 small onion, finely chopped

1 large carrot, chopped

2 garlic cloves, minced

2 teaspoons dried rosemary

1 teaspoon dried thyme

2 teaspoons kosher salt, plus more for seasoning

½ teaspoon freshly ground black pepper, plus more for seasoning

8 cups Chicken Stock (page 125)

Serves **8**
Prep time: **15 minutes**
Cook time: **8 hours (Low)**
DAIRY-FREE
NUT-FREE

Tip: Prepare the vegetables the night before to save time in the morning.

Per Serving (1 cup)
Calories: 97; Fat: 1g;
Protein: 6g;
Total Carbohydrates: 17g;
Fiber: 2g; Sugar: 1g;
Sodium: 310mg

1. In your slow cooker insert, stir together the chicken, wild rice, celery, onion, carrot, garlic, rosemary, thyme, salt, pepper, and chicken stock. Cover the cooker and cook on Low heat for 8 hours.

2. Remove the chicken. Using two forks, shred the chicken, then return it to the slow cooker. Stir to combine. Taste and season with more salt and pepper, as needed.

3. Refrigerate any leftovers in an airtight container or freeze for future use (see chart, page 12).

ENCHILADA SOUP

This enchilada soup is both filling and flavorful, just like the traditional dish that inspired it. I use just one large chicken breast, making this recipe budget friendly, too. If you like your soups chunkier, add a second chicken breast and double the enchilada sauce. Garnishes are always optional but encouraged: Fresh cilantro, shredded cheese, and tortilla strips are great options. If you're lucky enough to have leftovers, this makes a tasty next-day lunch.

1 large boneless, skinless chicken breast

2½ cups Chicken Stock (page 125)

1¼ cups Enchilada Sauce (page 129)

1 (15.25-ounce) can black beans, drained and rinsed

1 (10-ounce) can diced tomatoes with green chilies (I like Ro-Tel original brand)

1 garlic clove, minced

¼ onion, finely chopped

1 teaspoon kosher salt, plus more for seasoning

1 teaspoon ground cumin

Serves **4 to 6**
Prep time: **15 minutes**
Cook time: **8 hours (Low)**
DAIRY-FREE
NUT-FREE

Tip: To shred the chicken quickly, put the cooked chicken in the bowl of a stand mixer fitted with the paddle attachment and mix.

Per Serving (1 cup)
Calories: 170; Fat: 1g;
Protein: 16g;
Total Carbohydrates: 23g;
Fiber: 8g; Sugar: 4g;
Sodium: 650mg

1. In your slow cooker insert, stir together the chicken, chicken stock, enchilada sauce, black beans, tomatoes and green chilies with their juices, garlic, onion, salt, and cumin. Cover the cooker and cook on Low heat for 8 hours.

2. Remove the chicken breast. Using two forks, shred the chicken, then return it to the cooker. Stir to combine. Taste and add more salt, as needed. Serve warm with as many toppings as you'd like.

3. Refrigerate any leftovers in an airtight container or freeze for future use (see chart, page 12).

FRENCH ONION SOUP

Classic French onion soup seems fussy and difficult. It's not, but it does take time, which makes it a great option for the slow cooker. The hardest part is cutting the onions. If you have a mandoline, this is a great time to break it out. Not only will the slices be uniform, your eyes will thank you!

6 tablespoons (¾ stick) unsalted butter, at room temperature

2 pounds (about 5) white or yellow onions, thinly sliced

1 teaspoon sugar

1 tablespoon all-purpose flour

½ cup Marsala wine

5 cups Beef Stock (page 123)

1 teaspoon kosher salt, plus more for seasoning

½ teaspoon freshly ground black pepper, plus more for seasoning

½ loaf French bread, cut into slices

8 ounces grated Gruyère cheese

Serves **8**
Prep time: **15 minutes**
Cook time: **8 hours (Low)**
NUT-FREE

Tip: Try grated Comté, Swiss, or Gouda cheese if you cannot find Gruyère.

Per Serving (1 cup)
Calories: 315; Fat: 17g;
Protein: 11g;
Total Carbohydrates: 25g;
Fiber: 2g; Sugar: 9g;
Sodium: 321mg

1. Set your slow cooker to Low heat and add the butter to melt.

2. Stir in the onions and sugar. Cover the cooker and cook on Low heat for 8 hours.

3. Stir in the flour, wine, beef stock, and salt and pepper. Re-cover the cooker and cook until warmed through. Taste and add more salt and pepper, as needed.

4. While the soup warms, preheat the broiler.

5. Place the bread slices on a baking sheet. Broil briefly until toasted, keeping a careful eye on them to prevent burning. Leave the broiler on.

6. Line a rimmed baking sheet with a silicone mat and place 8 (16-ounce) ramekins or ovenproof bowls on the baking sheet. Ladle the soup into the ramekins. Top each bowl of soup with 1 slice of toasted bread and a sprinkling of cheese.

7. Carefully place the baking sheet in the oven and broil for 1 to 2 minutes or just until the cheese has melted, watching carefully to prevent burning. Serve immediately.

8. Refrigerate any leftovers in an airtight container or freeze for future use (see chart, page 12).

GUINNESS BEEF STEW

If you're in the mood for a stick-to-your-ribs kind of stew, Guinness beef stew is for you. Rich and hearty, this stew is filled with baby potatoes, carrots, and a sauce so good you'll want to be sure you have bread on hand to sop up every drop (an Irish soda bread would be quite fitting). If you prefer your sauce on the thicker side, stir in a cornstarch slurry at the end (see Tip, page 94).

1½ pounds beef stew meat

¼ cup all-purpose flour

1 teaspoon kosher salt, plus more for seasoning

¼ teaspoon freshly ground black pepper, plus more for seasoning

2 tablespoons extra-virgin olive oil

1 large onion, finely chopped

2 celery stalks, chopped

1 pound baby Dutch yellow potatoes

2 large carrots, cut into 2-inch pieces

1 (14.9-ounce) can Guinness beer

4 cups Beef Broth (page 122)

1 teaspoon dried thyme

3 tablespoons tomato paste

Serves **12**
Prep time: **15 minutes**
Cook time: **8 hours (Low)**
DAIRY-FREE
NUT-FREE

Tip: Prepare the veggies the night before for easier prep in the morning.

Per Serving (1 cup)
Calories: 158; Fat: 5g;
Protein: 14g;
Total Carbohydrates: 13g;
Fiber: 2g; Sugar: 2g;
Sodium: 160mg

1. In a large zip-top bag, combine the beef, flour, salt, and pepper. Seal the bag and shake to coat the beef.

2. In a heavy-bottomed pan over medium-high heat, heat the olive oil. Remove the beef from the bag and add it to the pan, working in batches if necessary. Cook until it is evenly browned and no longer pink. Transfer the browned meat to the slow cooker insert. Discard any excess flour.

3. Return the pan to the heat and add the onion and celery. Sauté until just softened. Add the vegetables to the slow cooker with the beef.

4. Stir in the potatoes, carrots, beer, beef broth, thyme, and tomato paste. Cover the cooker and cook on Low heat for 8 hours. Taste and add more salt and pepper, as needed.

5. Refrigerate any leftovers in an airtight container or freeze for future use (see chart, page 12).

ITALIAN VEAL STEW

Italian veal stew is perfect whenever you're craving comfort food. The stew meat is browned and then cooked slowly until tender in seasoned tomatoes, stock, and Marsala wine. The Italian-style tomatoes make this dish extra easy, eliminating the need for extra spices. For a fancier twist, serve this stew over a bed of polenta with a sprinkling of chopped fresh parsley.

1½ pounds veal stew meat

½ cup all-purpose flour

1 teaspoon kosher salt, plus more for seasoning

½ teaspoon freshly ground black pepper, plus more for seasoning

1 tablespoon extra-virgin olive oil

2 carrots, chopped

1 small onion, finely chopped

1 celery stalk, chopped

2 garlic cloves, minced

½ cup Marsala wine

1 (14.5-ounce) can Italian-style tomatoes

2 (8-ounce) cans tomato sauce

2 cups Beef Broth (page 122)

Serves **8**
Prep time: **15 minutes**
Cook time: **8 hours (Low)**
DAIRY-FREE
NUT-FREE

Tips: Prepare the vegetables the night before to save time in the morning. A food processor can help you quickly prep such items as onion, carrots, celery, and garlic.

Per Serving (1 cup)
Calories: 193; Fat: 4g;
Protein: 19g;
Total Carbohydrates: 15g;
Fiber: 3g; Sugar: 6g;
Sodium: 558mg

1. In a large zip-top bag, combine the stew meat, flour, salt, and pepper. Seal the bag and shake to coat the veal.

2. In a heavy-bottomed pan over medium-high heat, heat the olive oil. Remove the veal from the bag and add it to the pan, working in batches if necessary. Cook until it is evenly browned and no longer pink. Transfer the browned meat to the slow cooker insert. Discard any excess flour.

3. Return the pan to the heat and add the carrots, onion, celery, and garlic. Sauté until just softened.

4. Carefully stir the Marsala into the pan, scraping up the browned bits from the bottom of the pan to deglaze it. Transfer the veggies and wine to the slow cooker insert.

5. Stir in the tomatoes with their juices, tomato sauce, and beef broth. Cover the cooker and cook on Low heat for 8 hours. Taste and season with more salt and pepper, as needed.

6. Refrigerate any leftovers in an airtight container or freeze for future use (see chart, page 12).

BROCCOLI CHEDDAR SOUP

Broccoli Cheddar is a classic soup. Choose prepackaged broccoli florets for convenience or purchase a head of broccoli and cut it yourself to save a little money. The soup's consistency is all about your preference. Like it smoother? Puree longer. Like a little texture? Puree less and leave a few intact florets for good measure. Want the soup thicker? Add a little cornstarch slurry (see Tip, page 94). It's good to have options.

4 cups fresh
broccoli florets

2 carrots, chopped

1 garlic clove, minced

1 shallot, chopped

1 teaspoon kosher salt,
plus more for seasoning

6 cups Chicken Stock
(page 125)

1 cup heavy
(whipping) cream

8 ounces shredded
Cheddar cheese

Serves **10**
Prep time: **15 minutes**
Cook time: **8 hours (Low)**
NUT-FREE

Tips: If you can't find shallots at your grocery store, substitute ¼ cup of chopped yellow onion. Prep the vegetables the night before for added convenience.

Per Serving (1 cup)
Calories: 193; Fat: 17g;
Protein: 7g;
Total Carbohydrates: 5g;
Fiber: 1g; Sugar: 2g;
Sodium: 321mg

1. In your slow cooker insert, stir together the broccoli, carrots, garlic, shallot, salt, and chicken stock. Cover the cooker and cook on Low heat for 8 hours.

2. Taste and add more salt, as needed.

3. Using an immersion blender, blend the soup in the cooker until it reaches your desired consistency. Or, transfer the soup to a standard blender, in batches as needed, and blend as desired. Return the soup to the slow cooker insert.

4. Stir in the heavy cream. Slowly add the cheese, stirring as you go to make sure it melts evenly and does not clump.

5. Refrigerate any leftovers in an airtight container or freeze for future use (see chart, page 12).

LENTIL SOUP

Lentils are nutritious, budget friendly, and packed with protein, making them an excellent Meatless Monday dinner choice. This soup is full of flavor thanks to its rich tomato-based broth, which only gets tastier the next day. Top your bowl with a grating of Parmesan (if you don't need the soup to be vegan) and serve with a slice of toasted baguette for dipping, or add a side salad for a complete meal.

2 carrots, chopped

2 celery stalks, chopped

1 small onion, finely chopped

½ cup small green lentils, rinsed

2 garlic cloves, minced

2 bay leaves

1 tablespoon extra-virgin olive oil

2 teaspoons kosher salt, plus more for seasoning

½ teaspoon ground cumin

¼ teaspoon freshly ground black pepper, plus more for seasoning

1 (14.5-ounce) can diced tomatoes

4 cups Vegetable Broth (page 127)

Serves **6**
Prep time: **15 minutes**
Cook time: **8 hours (Low)**
DAIRY-FREE
NUT-FREE
VEGAN

Tip: Prepare the vegetables the night before to save time in the morning.

Per Serving (1 cup)
Calories: 103; Fat: 3g;
Protein: 5g;
Total Carbohydrates: 16g;
Fiber: 4g; Sugar: 4g;
Sodium: 549mg

1. In your slow cooker insert, stir together the carrots, celery, onion, lentils, garlic, bay leaves, olive oil, salt, cumin, pepper, tomatoes with their juices, and vegetable broth. Cover the cooker and cook on Low heat for 8 hours.

2. Remove and discard the bay leaves. Taste and add more salt and pepper, as needed.

3. Refrigerate any leftovers in an airtight container or freeze for future use (see chart, page 12).

MINESTRONE

Minestrone is the ultimate vegetable soup. Its beauty is that you can substitute whatever veggies you have on hand. No green beans? Try lima beans. The Parmesan rind adds depth and flavor to the broth. Whenever I get to the end of a Parmesan wedge, I cut the rind into smaller pieces and freeze to have them handy to use in soups.

1 (14.5-ounce) can diced tomatoes

2 carrots, chopped

2 celery stalks, chopped

2 potatoes, peeled and diced

1 small onion, finely chopped

2 garlic cloves, minced

4 cups Vegetable Broth (page 127)

2 cups water

2 bay leaves

2 teaspoons kosher salt, plus more for seasoning

1 teaspoon Italian seasoning

¼ teaspoon freshly ground black pepper, plus more for seasoning

1-inch piece Parmesan rind

1 cup trimmed, halved fresh green beans

Serves **10**
Prep time: **15 minutes**
Cook time: **8 hours (Low)**
NUT-FREE
VEGETARIAN

Tip: Prepare the vegetables the night before to save time in the morning.

Per Serving (1 cup)
Calories: 76; Fat: 0g;
Protein: 2g;
Total Carbohydrates: 17g;
Fiber: 3g; Sugar: 3g;
Sodium: 412mg

1. In your slow cooker insert, stir together the tomatoes with their juices, carrots, celery, potatoes, onion, garlic, vegetable broth, water, bay leaves, salt, Italian seasoning, pepper, Parmesan rind, and green beans. Cover the cooker and cook on Low heat for 8 hours.

2. Remove and discard the bay leaves and Parmesan rind. Taste and add more salt and pepper, as needed.

3. Refrigerate any leftovers in an airtight container or freeze for future use (see chart, page 12).

POTATO SOUP

Potato soup is creamy, dreamy, and totally customizable. You decide on the consistency by how much you mash: for a chunky soup, not much mashing; for smooth, go to town. The soup is great on its own but even better with a plethora of toppings. Simply add shredded Cheddar cheese, bacon bits, sliced scallions, and voilà—loaded baked potato soup.

5 pounds potatoes, peeled and chopped

6 cups Chicken Stock (page 125)

2 teaspoons kosher salt, plus more for seasoning

½ teaspoon freshly ground black pepper, plus more for seasoning

¼ teaspoon garlic powder

½ cup heavy (whipping) cream

2 tablespoons unsalted butter

1 teaspoon cornstarch

Serves **6**
Prep time: **15 minutes**
Cook time: **8 hours (Low)**
NUT-FREE

Tip: To save time, prep your potatoes the night before. Once peeled and diced, place them in a sealable container, cover with water, and refrigerate overnight. Discard the water before using the potatoes.

Per Serving (1 cup)
Calories: 396; Fat: 11g;
Protein: 8g;
Total Carbohydrates: 67g;
Fiber: 8g; Sugar: 4g;
Sodium: 418mg

1. In your slow cooker insert, stir together the potatoes, chicken stock, salt, pepper, and garlic powder. Cover the cooker and cook on Low heat for 8 hours.

2. Using a potato masher, mash the potatoes to your desired consistency. Add the heavy cream and butter. Mix to combine.

3. In a small bowl, whisk the cornstarch with a few tablespoons of the soup mixture until dissolved. Return the slurry to the slow cooker and stir to combine. Taste and add more salt and pepper, as needed. Serve the soup with toppings, as desired.

4. Refrigerate any leftovers in an airtight container or freeze for future use (see chart, page 12).

SAUSAGE, WHITE BEAN, AND COLLARDS SOUP

Collards (or collard greens) are a staple side dish in the South and have always been a part of my New Year's Day meal tradition. This soup is a riff on that supercharged side, and it hits the spot any time of year. Garnish this hearty soup with a grating of fresh Parmesan for a little extra richness.

1 pound ground mild Italian sausage

1 shallot, chopped

1 pound collards, rinsed, stemmed, and roughly chopped (see tip)

8 cups Chicken Stock (page 125)

2 tablespoons apple cider vinegar

2 teaspoons kosher salt, plus more for seasoning

¼ teaspoon freshly ground black pepper, plus more for seasoning

1 (15.5-ounce) can cannellini beans, drained and rinsed

Serves **14**
Prep time: **15 minutes**
Cook time: **8 hours (Low)**
DAIRY-FREE
NUT-FREE

Tip: To clean fresh collards, rinse them first, then remove the long stem that runs down the middle of each leaf; a sharp knife does the trick nicely. Once the stems are removed, stack the leaves, roll them, and give them a rough chop. Alternatively, use prepackaged chopped collards for convenience.

Per Serving (1 cup)
Calories: 148; Fat: 10g;
Protein: 7g;
Total Carbohydrates: 6g;
Fiber: 3g; Sugar: 0g;
Sodium: 409mg

1. In a skillet over medium-high heat, cook the ground sausage, breaking it up with a spoon, until it is browned and no longer pink. Drain off any excess fat and transfer the sausage to your slow cooker insert.

2. Add the shallot, collards, chicken stock, vinegar, salt, pepper, and beans. The pot will be quite full. Press down the collards as far as possible. They will wilt significantly as they cook. Cover the cooker and cook on Low heat for 8 hours. Taste and add more salt and pepper, as needed.

3. Refrigerate any leftovers in an airtight container or freeze for future use (see chart, page 12).

SWEET POTATO AND BLACK BEAN CHILI

When you're craving chili but want it with a twist, try this sweet potato and black bean version. It's full of bold spices that pair well with the starchiness of the sweet potatoes and black beans and is great on its own or over a bed of rice. Brighten it up with a handful of chopped fresh cilantro.

1 (15.5-ounce) can black beans, drained and rinsed

1 small onion, finely chopped

3 garlic cloves, minced

3 small sweet potatoes, peeled and cut into ½-inch dice

2 (14.5-ounce) cans diced tomatoes

3 tablespoons chili powder

1 teaspoon ground cumin

1 teaspoon kosher salt, plus more for seasoning

1 teaspoon sugar

½ teaspoon ground cinnamon

1 cup Vegetable Broth (page 127)

Serves **8**
Prep time: **15 minutes**
Cook time: **8 hours (Low)**
DAIRY-FREE
NUT-FREE
VEGAN

Tip: Prepare the vegetables the night before to save time in the morning.

Per Serving (1 cup)
Calories: 148; Fat: 10g;
Protein: 7g;
Total Carbohydrates: 6g;
Fiber: 3g; Sugar: 0g;
Sodium: 409mg

1. In your slow cooker insert, combine the black beans, onion, garlic, sweet potatoes, tomatoes with their juices, chili powder, cumin, salt, sugar, cinnamon, and vegetable broth. Cover the cooker and cook on Low heat for 8 hours. Taste and add more salt, as needed.

2. Refrigerate any leftovers in an airtight container or freeze for future use (see chart, page 12).

TACO SOUP

Let's taco 'bout this soup! It's your favorite Tuesday tradition in a soup; beef, spices, beans, and broth give you all your favorite familiar taco flavors but in an extra-hearty form. Because the best tacos are dressed up, top your bowl with shredded cheese, sliced avocado, or even tortilla strips. This recipe makes a large batch, so freeze some for your next Taco Tuesday, too.

1 tablespoon extra-virgin olive oil

1 pound ground beef

1 (15.5-ounce) can kidney beans, drained and rinsed

1 (15.5-ounce) can pinto beans, drained and rinsed

2 (14.5 ounce) cans diced tomatoes

1 (10-ounce) can diced tomatoes with green chilies (I like Ro-Tel original brand)

1 (8-ounce) can tomato sauce

2 tablespoons chili powder

1 teaspoon ground cumin

1 teaspoon garlic powder

1 teaspoon kosher salt

½ teaspoon smoked paprika

½ teaspoon dried oregano

½ onion powder

2 cups Beef Broth (page 122)

Serves **10**
Prep time: **15 minutes**
Cook time: **8 hours (Low)**
DAIRY-FREE
NUT-FREE

Tip: Measure the spices and brown the meat the night before and refrigerate in a sealed container to save time in the morning.

Per Serving (1 cup)
Calories: 175; Fat: 5g;
Protein: 16g;
Total Carbohydrates: 20g;
Fiber: 7g; Sugar: 4g;
Sodium: 415mg

1. In a heavy-bottomed pan over medium heat, heat the olive oil. Add the beef and cook, breaking up the meat with a spoon, until it is evenly browned and no longer pink. Drain off any excess fat. Transfer the beef to your slow cooker insert.

2. Stir in the kidney beans, pinto beans, tomatoes with their juices, tomatoes with green chilies, tomato sauce, chili powder, cumin, garlic powder, salt, paprika, oregano, onion powder, and beef broth. Cover the cooker and cook on Low heat for 8 hours.

3. Refrigerate any leftovers in an airtight container or freeze for future use (see chart, page 12).

THAI-INSPIRED COCONUT SOUP WITH CHICKEN

This soup is big, bold, and full of flavor. I prefer this soup on the brothy side, but if you want it a little heartier, add a second chicken breast. A squeeze of lime juice and generous heaping of chopped fresh cilantro when serving add an extra punch of bright flavor. Check the refrigerated produce section for tubes of ginger and garlic pastes, and the international aisle for red curry paste.

1 boneless, skinless chicken breast

5 cups Chicken Stock (page 125)

2 tablespoons ginger paste

1 tablespoon garlic paste

3 tablespoons red curry paste

2 (13.5-ounce) cans unsweetened coconut milk (shake well before using)

2 ounces mushrooms, thinly sliced

Serves **8**
Prep time: **15 minutes**
Cook time: **8 hours, 15 minutes (Low)**
DAIRY-FREE

Tip: Use a mandoline to slice the mushrooms thinly, quickly, and evenly.

Per Serving (1 cup)
Calories: 226; Fat: 21g;
Protein: 8g;
Total Carbohydrates: 5g;
Fiber: 1g; Sugar: 0g;
Sodium: 68mg

1. In your slow cooker insert, stir together the chicken, chicken stock, ginger paste, garlic paste, and curry paste. Cover the cooker and cook on Low heat for 8 hours.

2. Remove the chicken and, using two forks, shred it. Set aside.

3. Add the coconut milk and mushrooms to the slow cooker and stir to combine.

4. Stir in the shredded chicken. Re-cover the cooker and cook for 15 minutes more.

5. Refrigerate any leftovers in an airtight container or freeze for future use (see chart, page 12).

TURKEY, BLACK BEAN, AND PUMPKIN CHILI

This recipe calls for pumpkin puree, not pumpkin pie filling, so be careful when shopping not to pick up the sweet treat by accident. This chili is hearty on its own but, to make the meal even more substantial, consider serving the chili over a bed of rice.

1 tablespoon extra-virgin olive oil

1 pound lean ground turkey

1 (15-ounce) can pumpkin puree

1 (15-ounce) can black beans, drained and rinsed

1 (14.5-ounce) can diced tomatoes

2 cups water

3 tablespoons chili powder

1 teaspoon ground cumin

1 teaspoon ground cinnamon

1 teaspoon kosher salt, plus more for seasoning

1 teaspoon freshly ground black pepper, plus more for seasoning

½ teaspoon onion powder

¼ teaspoon cayenne pepper

¼ teaspoon ground cloves

Serves **8**
Prep time: **15 minutes**
Cook time: **8 hours (Low)**
DAIRY-FREE
NUT-FREE

Tip: Brown the turkey and refrigerate it the night before for quicker prep in the morning.

Per Serving (1 cup)
Calories: 180; Fat: 7g;
Protein: 15g;
Total Carbohydrates: 16g;
Fiber: 7g; Sugar: 3g;
Sodium: 333mg

1. In a heavy-bottomed pan over medium heat, heat the olive oil until shimmering. Add the turkey and cook, breaking up the meat with a spoon, until it is evenly browned and no longer pink. Drain off any excess fat and transfer the turkey to your slow cooker insert.

2. Stir in the pumpkin, black beans, tomatoes with their juices, water, chili powder, cumin, cinnamon, salt, black pepper, onion powder, cayenne, and cloves. Cover the cooker and cook on Low heat for 8 hours. Taste and add more salt and pepper, as needed.

3. Refrigerate any leftovers in an airtight container or freeze for future use (see chart, page 12).

WHITE CHICKEN CHILI

White chicken chili is one of my favorite dishes. It's rich, thick, decadent, and perfect for when you're craving comfort food. The heat from the jalapeño adds a delightful kick; if you like it even hotter, add an additional jalapeño. I recommend wearing gloves when handling jalapeños, and remember not to rub your eyes!

2 boneless, skinless chicken breasts

2 (15.5-ounce) cans cannellini beans, drained and rinsed

1 (15.25-ounce) can corn kernels, drained

1 small onion, finely chopped

2 garlic cloves, minced

1 jalapeño pepper, seeded, ribbed, and minced

4 cups Chicken Stock (page 125)

3 teaspoons ground cumin

1 teaspoon kosher salt, plus more for seasoning

1 teaspoon dried oregano

4 ounces cream cheese, at room temperature

Serves **10**
Prep time: **15 minutes**
Cook time: **8 hours (Low)**
NUT-FREE

Tips: Prepare the vegetables the night before to save time in the morning. You can also substitute store-bought low-sodium chicken stock for the homemade stock.

Per Serving (1 cup)
Calories: 169; Fat: 5g;
Protein: 13g;
Total Carbohydrates: 19g;
Fiber: 5g; Sugar: 2g;
Sodium: 238mg

1. In your slow cooker insert, stir together the chicken, beans, corn, onion, garlic, jalapeño, chicken stock, cumin, salt, and oregano. Cover the cooker and cook on Low heat for 8 hours.

2. Remove the chicken and, using two forks, shred it, then return it to the cooker.

3. Add the cream cheese to the slow cooker. Stir to melt and combine. Taste and season with more salt, as needed.

4. Refrigerate any leftovers in an airtight container or freeze for future use (see chart, page 12).

BEEF AND BARLEY STEW

Stew meat is budget friendly and perfectly suited for slow cooking—the hours spent braising take it from tough to tender. Beef and barley is a classic combination and ideal for a cold weather day. The sauce develops a gravy-like consistency that you'll want every drop of, be it by raking a cube of meat through it or running a piece of hearty bread across your plate.

1 tablespoon extra-virgin olive oil

1½ pounds beef stew meat

2 teaspoons kosher salt, plus more for seasoning

½ teaspoon freshly ground black pepper, plus more for seasoning

2 or 3 carrots, finely chopped

1 small onion, finely chopped

3 garlic cloves, minced

¾ cup pearl barley

1 cup red wine

5 cups Beef Broth (page 122)

1 (6-ounce) can tomato paste

1 tablespoon Worcestershire sauce

2 bay leaves

Serves **8**
Prep time: **15 minutes**
Cook time: **8 hours (Low)**
DAIRY-FREE
NUT-FREE

Tip: Prepare the vegetables the night before to save time in the morning.

Per Serving (1 cup)
Calories: 242; Fat: 5g;
Protein: 22g;
Total Carbohydrates: 23g;
Fiber: 4g; Sugar: 4g;
Sodium: 406mg

1. In a heavy-bottomed pan over medium heat, heat the olive oil. Season the beef with the salt and pepper, then add it to the pan, working in batches if necessary. Cook until the beef is evenly browned and no longer pink, then transfer it to your slow cooker insert.

2. Stir in the carrots, onion, garlic, barley, red wine, beef broth, tomato paste, Worcestershire sauce, and bay leaves. Cover the cooker and cook on Low heat for 8 hours.

3. Remove and discard the bay leaves. Taste and add more salt and pepper, as needed.

4. Refrigerate any leftovers in an airtight container or freeze for future use (see chart, page 12).

HUNGARIAN-INSPIRED PORK STEW

This stew's flavor runs deep, thanks to the Worcestershire sauce and sweet Hungarian paprika. It is delicious served over rice or egg noodles. If you're feeling a little extra, mix in a tablespoon or two of sour cream before serving and garnish with a sprinkling of chopped fresh parsley. If your local grocery store doesn't carry sweet Hungarian paprika, use a conventional smoked variety instead.

1½ pounds pork stew meat

1 large onion, finely chopped

2 garlic cloves, minced

1 (6-ounce) can tomato paste

4 to 5 cups Chicken Stock (page 125)

1 tablespoon Worcestershire sauce

2 teaspoons kosher salt, plus more for seasoning

1 teaspoon sweet Hungarian paprika

Serves **6**
Prep time: **15 minutes**
Cook time: **8 hours (Low)**
DAIRY-FREE
NUT-FREE

Tip: Prepare the vegetables the night before to save time in the morning.

Per Serving (1 cup)
Calories: 188; Fat: 5g;
Protein: 27g;
Total Carbohydrates: 9g;
Fiber: 2g; Sugar: 5g;
Sodium: 489mg

1. In your slow cooker insert, stir together the pork, onion, garlic, tomato paste, 4 cups of chicken stock, Worcestershire sauce, salt, and paprika. If the pork is not submerged, add the remaining 1 cup of stock. Cover the cooker and cook on Low heat for 8 hours.

2. Taste and add more salt, as needed.

3. Refrigerate any leftovers in an airtight container or freeze for future use (see chart, page 12).

MOROCCAN-INSPIRED LAMB STEW

Lamb stew meat is slow-cooked to tender perfection with a bold-flavored Moroccan seasoning blend called ras el hanout. The blend includes warming spices such as cinnamon, cumin, coriander, peppers, turmeric, and more. Serve this stew over a bed of couscous and garnish it with a heaping handful of chopped fresh parsley and a grating of lemon zest for extra flavor.

1½ pounds lamb stew meat

2 carrots, chopped

1 small onion, finely chopped

1 (6-ounce) can tomato paste

2 tablespoons ras el hanout (I like McCormick brand Moroccan seasoning)

1 teaspoon kosher salt, plus more for seasoning

½ teaspoon garlic powder

3 cups water

Serves **8**
Prep time: **15 minutes**
Cook time: **8 hours (Low)**
DAIRY-FREE
NUT-FREE

Per Serving (1 cup)
Calories: 142; Fat: 5g;
Protein: 18g;
Total Carbohydrates: 6g;
Fiber: 2g; Sugar: 4g;
Sodium: 224mg

1. In your slow cooker insert, stir together the lamb, carrots, onion, tomato paste, ras el hanout, salt, garlic powder, and water. Cover the cooker and cook on Low heat for 8 hours.

2. Taste and add more salt, as needed.

3. Refrigerate any leftovers in an airtight container or freeze for future use (see chart, page 12).

BLACK BEAN SOUP

Black bean soup can be thick and rich, or brothy and chunky—it's all about how much of it you puree. Can't decide? Puree half the soup to create a half-and-half bowl of beany bliss. I love to load this soup with garnishes because, let's face it, it's not the prettiest soup around, but what it lacks in looks it makes up for in flavor. Some optional toppings I like are chopped avocado, chopped fresh cilantro, or shredded cheese.

1 pound dried black beans, rinsed

6 cups Vegetable Broth (page 127)

1 (14.5-ounce) can diced tomatoes

1 small onion, finely chopped

1 red bell pepper, finely chopped

2 garlic cloves, minced

2 teaspoons chili powder

2 teaspoons ground cumin

2 teaspoons kosher salt, plus more for seasoning

1 bay leaf

½ teaspoon freshly ground black pepper, plus more for seasoning

Serves **10**
Prep time: **15 minutes**
Cook time: **8 to 10 hours (Low)**
DAIRY-FREE
NUT-FREE
VEGAN

Tips: If the soup is too thick, thin it with additional vegetable broth until it reaches your desired consistency. If you don't have an immersion blender, use a traditional blender, working in batches if necessary, or a potato masher.

Per Serving (1 cup)
Calories: 172; Fat: 1g;
Protein: 11g;
Total Carbohydrates: 32g;
Fiber: 8g; Sugar: 3g;
Sodium: 299mg

1. In your slow cooker insert, stir together the black beans, vegetable broth, tomatoes with their juices, onion, red bell pepper, garlic, chili powder, cumin, salt, bay leaf, and pepper. Cover the cooker and cook on Low heat for 8 to 10 hours or until the beans are soft enough to puree.

2. Remove and discard the bay leaf. Using an immersion blender, puree the soup until it reaches your desired consistency. Taste and add more salt and pepper, as needed.

3. Refrigerate any leftovers in an airtight container or freeze for future use (see chart, page 12).

PASTA E FAGIOLI SOUP

Pasta e fagioli simply means pasta and beans—it doesn't get much more budget friendly than that. If you like a thicker soup, puree half the soup and stir it back into the pot before adding the pasta. If you prefer a thinner soup, add an extra splash of broth at the end, to compensate for the pasta drinking up the cooking liquid. Chopped fresh parsley, a grating of Pecorino-Romano, and a drizzle of olive oil make the perfect finishing touches.

1 (28-ounce) can crushed tomatoes

4 cups Vegetable Broth (page 127)

2 cups water

1 (15.5-ounce) can pinto beans, or cannellini beans, drained and rinsed

2 celery stalks, chopped

2 carrots, chopped

1 small onion, finely chopped

3 garlic cloves, minced

1 tablespoon extra-virgin olive oil

1 teaspoon kosher salt, plus more for seasoning

¼ teaspoon freshly ground black pepper, plus more for seasoning

¼ teaspoon red pepper flakes

1 cup ditalini, or other small pasta

Serves **12**
Prep time: **15 minutes**
Cook time: **8 hours (Low)**
DAIRY-FREE
NUT-FREE
VEGAN

Tip: Prepare the vegetables the night before to save time in the morning.

Per Serving (1 cup)
Calories: 106; Fat: 2g;
Protein: 4g;
Total Carbohydrates: 20g;
Fiber: 4g; Sugar: 4g;
Sodium: 128mg

1. In your slow cooker insert, stir together the tomatoes, vegetable broth, water, pinto beans, celery, carrots, onion, garlic, olive oil, salt, black pepper, and red pepper flakes. Cover the cooker and cook on Low heat for 8 hours.

2. Taste and add more salt and pepper, as needed.

3. Stir in the pasta. Re-cover the cooker and cook 5 to 10 minutes more or until the pasta is al dente.

4. Refrigerate any leftovers in an airtight container or freeze for future use (see chart, page 12).

CHEESY BLACK BEAN
AND CORN ENCHILADAS, 46

CHAPTER THREE

VEGETARIAN AND VEGAN

CHEESY BLACK BEAN AND CORN ENCHILADAS

This casserole comes together quickly with just a little prep the night before. Mix the filling in advance, so all that's left to do in the morning is roll and stack the enchiladas. I found that corn tortillas did not hold up as well as flour ones during the longer cooking process, so I do not suggest substituting them. These enchiladas are great topped with sliced jalapeños, sour cream, chopped fresh cilantro, and even additional cheese.

1 onion, finely chopped

1 (15-ounce) can black beans, drained and rinsed

1 (15.25-ounce) can corn kernels, drained

1 tablespoon chili powder

1 teaspoon ground cumin

1 teaspoon kosher salt

1½ cups shredded Mexican cheese blend, divided

Nonstick cooking spray

3 cups Enchilada Sauce (page 129), divided, plus more as needed

10 small flour tortillas

Serves **5**
Prep time: **15 minutes**
Cook time: **8 hours (Low)**
NUT-FREE
VEGETARIAN

Tip: Make sure the tortillas are completely covered with the sauce. If they are not, add more sauce until they are.

Per Serving (2 enchiladas)
Calories: 413; Fat: 15g;
Protein: 18g;
Total Carbohydrates: 56g;
Fiber: 11g; Sugar: 11g;
Sodium: 1436mg

1. In a medium bowl, stir together the onion, black beans, corn, chili powder, cumin, salt, and 1 cup of cheese.

2. Coat the slow cooker insert with cooking spray.

3. Pour 1 cup of enchilada sauce into the bottom of the prepared insert.

4. Place the tortillas on a work surface. Place ½ cup of the black bean mixture into the middle of a tortilla and roll it up. Place the enchilada, seam-side down, in the slow cooker insert. Repeat this step until you have a row of 5 enchiladas.

5. Pour 1 cup of enchilada sauce over the row of enchiladas, making sure the surface of the tortillas is covered.

6. Repeat step 4 with the remaining 5 tortillas and black bean filling. Pour the remaining 1 cup of enchilada sauce over the enchiladas. Cover the cooker and cook on Low heat for 8 hours.

7. Top the enchiladas with the remaining ½ cup of cheese. Re-cover the cooker and allow the cheese to quickly melt.

8. Refrigerate any leftovers in an airtight container or freeze for future use (see chart, page 12).

CALABACITAS

Calabacitas (literally "little squash") is a popular New Mexican dish full of corn, peppers, squash, and tomatoes. This dish can be eaten as is, but if you want to go the extra mile, finish it with a handful of shredded Cheddar cheese. Just cover the cooker with its lid and give the cheese a minute or two to melt. Then, for a little freshness, add a sprinkling of chopped fresh cilantro and sliced scallion. Delish!

1 (15.25-ounce) can corn kernels, drained

2 zucchini, cut into ½-inch dice

1 small onion, finely chopped

1 (14.5-ounce) can diced tomatoes

8 ounces tomato sauce

1 jalapeño pepper, seeded and minced

1 teaspoon dried oregano

1 teaspoon kosher salt, plus more for seasoning

Serves **8**
Prep time: **15 minutes**
Cook time: **8 hours (Low)**
DAIRY-FREE
NUT-FREE
VEGAN

Tip: Substitute yellow crookneck squash for the zucchini.

Per Serving (1 cup)
Calories: 58; Fat: 1g;
Protein: 2g;
Total Carbohydrates: 12g;
Fiber: 3g; Sugar: 5g;
Sodium: 422mg

1. In your slow cooker insert, stir together the corn, zucchini, onion, tomatoes with their juices, tomato sauce, jalapeño, oregano, and salt. Cover the cooker and cook on Low heat for 8 hours. Taste and add more salt, as needed.

2. Refrigerate any leftovers in an airtight container or freeze for future use (see chart, page 12).

CHICKPEA CURRY

I'm always eager to grab a second bowl of this curry; its warming spices just hit the spot. Its heat level is on the mild side, but you can choose to add an extra tablespoon or two of red curry paste at the end for extra kick. Want more veggies? Add a handful or two of fresh spinach at the end and cook just until wilted. Serve this curry with naan or over a bed of basmati rice, and garnish with chopped fresh cilantro.

2 (15.5-ounce) cans chickpeas, drained and rinsed

2 (14.5-ounce) cans diced tomatoes

1 onion, finely chopped

1 (13.5-ounce) can coconut milk (shake well before opening)

1 cup water

4 garlic cloves, minced

1 tablespoon extra-virgin olive oil

1 tablespoon garam masala

1 tablespoon red curry paste (I like Thai Kitchen), plus more for seasoning

½ teaspoon ground ginger

Serves **8**
Prep time: **15 minutes**
Cook time: **8 hours (Low)**
DAIRY-FREE
VEGAN

Tip: Look for red curry paste in the international aisle of most grocery stores.

Per Serving (1 cup)
Calories: 226; Fat: 14g;
Protein: 8g;
Total Carbohydrates: 22g;
Fiber: 7g; Sugar: 6g;
Sodium: 261mg

1. In your slow cooker insert; stir together the chickpeas, tomatoes with their juices, onion, coconut milk, water, garlic, olive oil, garam masala, red curry paste, and ginger. Cover the cooker and cook on Low heat for 8 hours.

2. Taste and add more red curry paste, as you like.

3. Refrigerate any leftovers in an airtight container or freeze for future use (see chart, page 12).

COCONUT LENTIL SOUP

This soup is wholesome, filling, delicious, and perfect on a chilly day. Small green lentils are slow cooked with aromatic spices and finished with coconut milk. If you're not familiar with garlic and ginger pastes, you can typically find them in tubes in the refrigerated section of most grocery stores. They're very convenient and you'll be surprised by how many times you use them.

1 cup small dried green lentils, rinsed

4 cups Vegetable Broth (page 127)

2 small carrots, finely chopped

1 small onion, finely chopped

1 celery stalk, finely chopped

1 teaspoon garlic paste

1 teaspoon ginger paste

1 teaspoon garam masala

1 teaspoon kosher salt, plus more for seasoning

1 (13.5-ounce) can coconut milk (shake well before opening)

Serves **8**
Prep time: **15 minutes**
Cook time: **8 hours (Low)**
DAIRY-FREE
VEGAN

Tip: Use a mini chopper or food processor to chop the carrots, onion, and celery.

Per Serving (1 cup)
Calories: 188; Fat: 11g;
Protein: 7g;
Total Carbohydrates: 19g;
Fiber: 3g; Sugar: 2g;
Sodium: 164mg

1. In your slow cooker insert, stir together the lentils, vegetable broth, carrots, onion, celery, garlic paste, ginger paste, garam masala, and salt. Cover the cooker and cook on Low heat for 8 hours.

2. Stir in the coconut milk. Re-cover the cooker and cook for 5 minutes more or until the coconut milk is just warmed through. Taste and add more salt, as needed.

3. Refrigerate any leftovers in an airtight container or freeze for future use (see chart, page 12).

RIBOLLITA

Ribollita is a hearty and homey Tuscan bean stew. Ribollita simply means "reboiled" in Italian, and yes, it's even better reheated the next day. The beauty of this stoup (stew-soup) is you can add anything you have on hand, such as spinach or kale. Just add them at the end with the bread, so the greens wilt in the heat of the stew. Garnish with a grating of Parmesan, if desired, and a drizzle of olive oil.

2 (15.5-ounce) cans cannellini beans, drained and rinsed

2 carrots, finely chopped

2 celery stalks, finely chopped

1 onion, finely chopped

3 garlic cloves, minced

1 (28-ounce) can crushed tomatoes

4 cups Vegetable Broth (page 127)

2 teaspoons kosher salt, plus more for seasoning

2 or 3 thyme sprigs

½ teaspoon red pepper flakes

2 cups cubed stale bread

Serves **10**
Prep time: **15 minutes**
Cook time: **8 hours (Low)**
NUT-FREE
VEGAN

Tip: Prepare the vegetables the night before to save time in the morning.

Per Serving (1 cup)
Calories: 107; Fat: 1g;
Protein: 6g;
Total Carbohydrates: 20g;
Fiber: 6g; Sugar: 4g;
Sodium: 366mg

1. In your slow cooker insert, stir together the cannellini beans, carrots, celery, onion, garlic, tomatoes, vegetable broth, salt, thyme, and red pepper flakes. Cover the cooker and cook on Low heat for 8 hours.

2. Remove and discard the thyme sprigs.

3. Stir in the bread. Re-cover the cooker and cook until the bread has softened, 1 to 2 minutes. Taste and add more salt, as needed.

4. Refrigerate any leftovers in an airtight container or freeze for future use (see chart, page 12).

RICE-STUFFED BELL PEPPERS

These rice-stuffed bell peppers are flavorful and filling. I prefer to use red, orange, and yellow bell peppers for their sweet taste, but use green bell peppers if you prefer. For the seasoning, look for Sazon in the international section of most grocery stores. To finish the peppers, I add a tablespoon of Enchilada Sauce (page 129) and additional shredded cheese to each pepper before serving.

6 to 8 bell peppers, any color, tops cut off and reserved, peppers seeded and ribbed

1 cup cooked rice

1 (15.5-ounce) can pinto beans, drained and rinsed

2 (0.17-ounce) packets Sazon seasoning

1 cup shredded Mexican cheese blend

1½ cups water

Serves **6 to 8**
Prep time: **15 minutes**
Cook time: **8 hours (Low)**
NUT-FREE
VEGETARIAN

Tip: Prepare the rice the night before to save time in the morning.

Per Serving (1 stuffed pepper)
Calories: 214; Fat: 6g;
Protein: 11g;
Total Carbohydrates: 31g;
Fiber: 6g; Sugar: 0g;
Sodium: 69mg

1. Place the peppers in the slow cooker insert, standing them upright. If needed, carefully trim a small slice off the bottom (being careful not to cut into the cavity) so the peppers won't fall over.

2. Remove and discard the stems from the reserved pepper tops. Finely chop the remaining pepper flesh from the tops.

3. In a medium bowl, stir together the cooked rice, pinto beans, seasoning, cheese, and chopped pepper tops. Fill the peppers with equal amounts of the rice mixture.

4. Pour the water around the peppers, being careful not to get any water inside them. Cover the cooker and cook on Low heat for 8 hours.

5. Refrigerate any leftovers in an airtight container or freeze for future use (see chart, page 12).

RICE-STUFFED CABBAGE ROLLS

Rice-stuffed cabbage rolls smothered in marinara sauce are perfect for a Meatless Monday meal. Rolling cabbage leaves may seem difficult, but it becomes exceptionally easy when you boil the cabbage leaves first, which makes them soft and pliable.

6 to 8 cabbage leaves

1 cup cooked rice

1 small onion,
finely chopped

2 garlic cloves, minced

1 tablespoon
Italian seasoning

1 teaspoon kosher salt

¼ teaspoon freshly
ground black pepper

1 large egg, beaten

3 cups Marinara Sauce
(page 130), divided, plus
more as needed

Serves **6 to 8**
Prep time: **15 minutes**
Cook time: **8 hours (Low)**
DAIRY-FREE
NUT-FREE
VEGETARIAN

Tips: Prepare the rice the night before to save time in the morning. Make sure the sauce completely covers the cabbage rolls; if it doesn't, add more sauce, as needed.

Per Serving (1 cabbage roll)
Calories: 99; Fat: 2g;
Protein: 5g;
Total Carbohydrates: 18g;
Fiber: 4g; Sugar: 6g;
Sodium: 571mg

1. Bring a large pot of water to a boil over high heat. Add the cabbage leaves and boil them for about 3 minutes or until soft. Remove the leaves and place on a work surface.

2. While the cabbage leaves cool, in a medium bowl, stir together the rice, onion, garlic, Italian seasoning, salt, pepper, and egg.

3. Pour 1 cup of marinara sauce into the bottom of your slow cooker insert.

4. Evenly divide the rice mixture among the cabbage leaves. Roll up each leaf around the filling, as you would roll a burrito. Place the rolls, seam-side down, into the slow cooker insert, stacking if needed.

5. Pour the remaining 2 cups of marinara sauce over the rolls. Cover the cooker and cook on Low heat for 8 hours.

6. Refrigerate any leftovers in an airtight container or freeze for future use (see chart, page 12).

ROOT VEGETABLE STEW

This stew is chock-full of carrots, potatoes, and parsnips. If you're not familiar with parsnips, they're a cream-colored, carrot-shaped root vegetable with a sweet flavor. You can usually find them in the produce section near the carrots. If you want your stew on the thicker side, add a cornstarch slurry at the end to thicken it quickly (see Tip, page 94). Serve the stew over rice and garnish with chopped fresh parsley.

2 parsnips, peeled and cut into 2-inch sections

2 carrots, peeled and cut into 2-inch sections

2 potatoes, peeled and chopped

2 celery stalks, finely chopped

1 onion, finely chopped

3 garlic cloves, minced

1 (14.5-ounce) can fire-roasted tomatoes

1 teaspoon kosher salt, plus more for seasoning

¼ teaspoon freshly ground black pepper, plus more for seasoning

Serves **10**
Prep time: **15 minutes**
Cook time: **8 hours (Low)**
DAIRY-FREE
NUT-FREE
VEGAN

Tips: Prepare the vegetables the night before to save time in the morning. You can also add 1 cup of peeled, cubed butternut squash to this stew.

Per Serving (1 cup)
Calories: 95; Fat: 0g;
Protein: 2g;
Total Carbohydrates: 22g;
Fiber: 3g; Sugar: 4g;
Sodium: 239mg

1. In your slow cooker insert, stir together the parsnips, carrots, potatoes, celery, onion, garlic, tomatoes with their juices, salt, and pepper. Cover the cooker and cook on Low heat for 8 hours. Taste and add more salt and pepper, as needed.

2. Refrigerate any leftovers in an airtight container or freeze for future use (see chart, page 12).

LOADED SLOW-COOKED SWEET POTATOES

Slow cooker sweet potatoes may just be the easiest recipe you'll make. Once you've washed and dried the sweet potatoes, they go into the slow cooker and cook until tender. You can comfortably fit 4 or 5 medium sweet potatoes in the cooker insert. When they're done, top them with a scoop of hearty chili. You can use store-bought chili or try the Sweet Potato and Black Bean Chili (page 33). For extra flair, top the cooked sweet potatoes with shredded cheese, sour cream, and chopped scallions, if desired.

4 or 5 sweet potatoes, washed and dried

1 (15-ounce) can vegetarian chili (such as Amy's Organic Vegan Chili)

Kosher salt

Toppings of choice (see headnote)

Serves **4 or 5**
Prep time: **5 minutes**
Cook time: **8 hours (Low)**
DAIRY-FREE
NUT-FREE
VEGAN

Per Serving (1 topped sweet potato)
Calories: 231; Fat: 6g;
Protein: 8g;
Total Carbohydrates: 39g;
Fiber: 9g; Sugar: 7g;
Sodium: 772mg

1. Put the sweet potatoes in your slow cooker insert. Cover the cooker and cook on Low heat for 8 hours.

2. Warm the chili in a pan on the stovetop. Slice the sweet potatoes lengthwise and season them with salt.

3. Serve the sweet potatoes topped with the chili and any other toppings you'd like.

4. Refrigerate any leftovers in an airtight container or freeze for future use (see chart, page 12).

SPLIT PEA DAL

If you're looking for something a little different from lentils, try this recipe. Split peas can usually be found with or near the dried beans in the grocery store. You can store leftover peas from your purchase in an air-tight container. I love to garnish this dal with a handful of chopped fresh cilantro and/or a dollop of sour cream and serve it over basmati rice or with naan.

1 cup dried green split peas, rinsed

4 cups Vegetable Broth (page 127)

1 (14.5-ounce) can fire-roasted diced tomatoes

1 small onion, finely chopped

3 garlic cloves, minced

1 tablespoon extra-virgin olive oil

1 teaspoon ground cumin

1 teaspoon ground coriander

2 teaspoons ground turmeric

2 teaspoons kosher salt, plus more for seasoning

¼ teaspoon cayenne pepper

Serves **8**
Prep time: **15 minutes**
Cook time: **8 hours (Low)**
DAIRY-FREE
NUT-FREE
VEGAN

Tip: Prepare the onion and garlic the night before to save time in the morning.

Per Serving (1 cup)
Calories: 118; Fat: 2g;
Protein: 7g;
Total Carbohydrates: 19g;
Fiber: 8g; Sugar: 4g;
Sodium: 355mg

1. In your slow cooker insert, stir together the split peas, vegetable broth, tomatoes with their juices, onion, garlic, olive oil, cumin, coriander, turmeric, salt, and cayenne. Cover the cooker and cook on Low heat for 8 hours. Taste and add more salt, as needed.

2. Refrigerate any leftovers in an airtight container or freeze for future use (see chart, page 12).

CORN CHOWDER

Rich and creamy corn chowder is perfect when fresh corn is in season. To save time, remove the kernels from the cobs the night before (see tip on how to do this in Corn Broth, page 126). Using the Corn Broth recipe in this book takes this chowder up a notch.

8 ears fresh corn on the cob, silks removed and husked

3 potatoes, peeled and cubed

½ small onion, finely chopped (about ¼ cup)

2 garlic cloves, minced

4 cups Corn Broth (page 126)

1 teaspoon kosher salt, plus more for seasoning

¼ teaspoon freshly ground black pepper, plus more for seasoning

¼ cup heavy (whipping) cream

Serves **8**
Prep time: **15 minutes**
Cook time: **8 hours (Low)**
NUT-FREE
VEGETARIAN

Tip: Vegetable broth can be used instead of corn broth.

Per Serving (1 cup)
Calories: 258; Fat: 4g;
Protein: 7g;
Total Carbohydrates: 54g;
Fiber: 7g; Sugar: 1g;
Sodium: 201mg

1. Remove the corn kernels from the cobs. Save the cobs to make Corn Broth (page 126). Put the kernels in your slow cooker insert and stir in the potatoes, onion, garlic, corn broth, salt, and pepper. Cover the cooker and cook on Low heat for 8 hours.

2. Using an immersion blender, blend the soup until smooth.

3. Stir in the heavy cream. Taste and add more salt and pepper, as needed.

4. Refrigerate any leftovers in an airtight container or freeze for future use (see chart, page 12).

LENTIL AND MUSHROOM BOLOGNESE

If you're looking for a vegan alternative to traditional meat-based Bolognese sauce, lentils and mushrooms make a great "meaty" substitute. A mini food processor or chopper comes in handy for this recipe and cuts down prep time. Serve this "Bolognese" over pasta, zoodles, or cauliflower gnocchi.

8 ounces baby bella mushrooms, finely chopped

2 celery stalks, finely chopped

2 carrots, finely chopped

1 small onion, finely chopped

2 garlic cloves, minced

1 cup small dried green lentils

1 cup Vegetable Broth (page 127)

½ cup red wine

2 ounces tomato paste

1 (28-ounce) can crushed tomatoes

2 bay leaves

2 teaspoons kosher salt, plus more for seasoning

¼ teaspoon freshly ground black pepper, plus more for seasoning

Serves **8**
Prep time: **15 minutes**
Cook time: **8 hours (Low)**
DAIRY-FREE
NUT-FREE
VEGAN

Tip: Prepare the vegetables the night before to save time in the morning.

Per Serving (1 cup)
Calories: 135; Fat: 1g;
Protein: 8g;
Total Carbohydrates: 24g;
Fiber: 6g; Sugar: 6g;
Sodium: 427mg

1. In your slow cooker insert, stir together the mushrooms, celery, carrots, onion, garlic, lentils, vegetable broth, red wine, tomato paste, tomatoes, bay leaves, salt, and pepper. Cover the cooker and cook on Low heat for 8 hours.

2. Remove and discard the bay leaves.

3. Taste and add more salt and pepper, as needed.

4. Refrigerate any leftovers in an airtight container or freeze for future use (see chart, page 12).

RED BEANS AND RICE

Red beans over steamed white rice is a classic and it couldn't be easier to make when you're using a slow cooker. This recipe starts with dried red beans that cook for hours in seasoned broth until tender. If you like, add a few dashes of hot sauce to kick it up. Corn bread makes a nice accompaniment for this dish.

1 pound small dried red beans, rinsed

2 celery stalks, finely chopped

1 small onion, finely chopped

1 red bell pepper, seeded and finely chopped

2 tablespoons chili powder

2 teaspoons ground cumin

1 teaspoon paprika

1 teaspoon kosher salt, plus more for seasoning

½ teaspoon cayenne pepper

5 cups Vegetable Broth (page 127)

Cooked white rice, for serving

Serve 8
Prep time: **15 minutes**
Cook time: **8 hours (Low)**
DAIRY-FREE
NUT-FREE
VEGAN

Tip: Prepare the vegetables and rice the night before to save time in the morning.

Per Serving (1 cup)
Calories: 209; Fat: 1g;
Protein: 13g;
Total Carbohydrates: 38g;
Fiber: 10g; Sugar: 2g;
Sodium: 304mg

1. In your slow cooker insert, stir together the beans, celery, onion, red bell pepper, chili powder, cumin, paprika, salt, cayenne, and vegetable broth. Cover the cooker and cook on Low heat for 8 hours. Taste and add more salt, as needed.

2. Serve the beans warm over the cooked rice.

3. Refrigerate any leftovers in an airtight container or freeze for future use (see chart, page 12).

SOUTHWEST BLACK BEAN AND CORN QUINOA

I believe even those who think they don't like quinoa will like this dish, and probably ask for seconds. This Southwestern-inspired quinoa is incredibly flavorful and brings a little kick without the burn. If you like to walk on the spicier side, add minced jalapeño to the mix. I like to sprinkle a handful of shredded Mexican blend cheese over the top at the end. Cover your cooker and let the cheese melt. Because I'm cheesy like that.

1 cup dried quinoa, rinsed

1 (15-ounce) can black beans, drained and rinsed

1 (15.25-ounce) can corn kernels, drained

1 (10-ounce) can diced tomatoes and green chilies (I like Ro-Tel original)

1 small onion, finely chopped

1 tablespoon chili powder

1 tablespoon Goya adobo seasoning

1 teaspoon ground cumin

4 cups Vegetable Broth (page 127)

Serves **8**
Prep time: **15 minutes**
Cook time: **8 hours (Low)**
DAIRY-FREE
NUT-FREE
VEGAN

Tip: Garnish with chopped fresh cilantro for a bright finish.

Per Serving (1 cup)
Calories: 166; Fat: 2g;
Protein: 8g;
Total Carbohydrates: 31g;
Fiber: 6g; Sugar: 2g;
Sodium: 456mg

1. In your slow cooker insert, stir together the quinoa, black beans, corn, tomatoes and green chilies with their juices, onion, chili powder, adobo seasoning, cumin, and vegetable broth. Cover the cooker and cook on Low heat for 8 hours.

2. Refrigerate any leftovers in an airtight container or freeze for future use (see chart, page 12).

SWEET POTATO CURRY

I am a sucker for all things curry powder. Spice is nice in my book. Note that this recipe uses curry powder, not curry paste. There is a difference, and a little goes a long way. If you don't have red onion on hand, substitute a yellow onion. You're going for a small bite-size dice on the sweet potatoes, and I recommend serving this curry over rice with a sprinkle of chopped fresh cilantro.

2 small sweet potatoes, peeled and cut into ½-inch dice

1 small red onion, finely chopped

1 teaspoon ginger paste

1 teaspoon garlic paste

1 teaspoon curry powder

½ teaspoon kosher salt

2 cups Vegetable Broth (page 127)

Serves **4**

Prep time: **15 minutes**

Cook time: **8 hours (Low)**

DAIRY-FREE

NUT-FREE

VEGAN

1. In your slow cooker insert, stir together the sweet potatoes, red onion, ginger paste, garlic paste, curry powder, salt, and vegetable broth. Cover the cooker and cook on Low heat for 8 hours. Taste and add more salt, as needed.

2. Refrigerate any leftovers in an airtight container or freeze for future use (see chart, page 12).

Tip: Prepare the vegetables the night before to save time in the morning.

Per Serving (1 cup)
Calories: 66; Fat: 0g;
Protein: 2g;
Total Carbohydrates: 15g;
Fiber: 3g; Sugar: 3g;
Sodium: 271mg

TOMATO BASIL SOUP

When I'm in the mood for soup, this one is high on my list. It reminds me of my childhood, and I simply cannot have a bowl of it without also having a grilled cheese sandwich on the side. Dunking is optional but encouraged. If you want a little luxury, add a splash of heavy cream to the soup at the end.

4 (14.5-ounce) cans diced tomatoes

1 small carrot, finely chopped

1 tablespoon minced shallot

1 teaspoon kosher salt, plus more for seasoning

¼ teaspoon freshly ground black pepper, plus more for seasoning

1 teaspoon dried basil

2 tablespoons unsalted butter

2 cups Vegetable Broth (page 127)

Serves **8**
Prep time: **15 minutes**
Cook time: **8 hours (Low)**
NUT-FREE
VEGETARIAN

Tip: Substitute yellow onion for the shallot.

Per Serving (1 cup)
Calories: 63; Fat: 4g;
Protein: 1g;
Total Carbohydrates: 9g;
Fiber: 4g; Sugar: 4g;
Sodium: 386mg

1. In your slow cooker insert, stir together the tomatoes with their juices, carrot, shallot, salt, pepper, basil, butter, and vegetable broth. Cover the cooker and cook on Low heat for 8 hours.

2. Using an immersion blender, puree the soup in the pot to your desired consistency, or transfer the soup to a standard blender and puree, in batches as needed. Taste and add more salt and pepper, as needed.

3. Refrigerate any leftovers in an airtight container or freeze for future use (see chart, page 12).

BUTTERNUT SQUASH SOUP

Butternut squash may seem intimidating to work with due to its unusual shape, but it's not. Start by cutting off a small portion of the top and bottom of the squash, just as you would a carrot. Then peel off the skin with a vegetable peeler. Halve the squash vertically and scoop out the seeds with a spoon. Cut the squash into cubes. It's as easy as that. This soup is surprisingly creamy without the addition of any actual cream, making it a fabulous vegan dinner option. For a little texture, garnish the soup with toasted croutons.

1 butternut squash, peeled, cleaned, and cubed (see headnote)

1 small onion, finely chopped

1 garlic clove, minced

1 teaspoon kosher salt, plus more for seasoning

¼ teaspoon freshly ground black pepper, plus more for seasoning

4 cups Vegetable Broth (page 127)

1 to 2 tablespoons pure maple syrup

½ teaspoon grated nutmeg

Serves **6**
Prep time: **15 minutes**
Cook time: **8 hours (Low)**
DAIRY-FREE
NUT-FREE
VEGAN

Tip: If the soup is too thick, add small amounts of additional vegetable broth until it reaches your desired consistency.

Per Serving (1 cup)
Calories: 76; Fat: 0g;
Protein: 1g;
Total Carbohydrates: 20g;
Fiber: 2g; Sugar: 7g;
Sodium: 316mg

1. In your slow cooker insert, stir together the squash, onion, garlic, salt, pepper, and vegetable broth. Cover the cooker and cook on Low heat for 8 hours.

2. Using an immersion blender, puree the soup in the pot until smooth.

3. Stir in the maple syrup and nutmeg. Taste and add more salt and pepper, as needed.

4. Refrigerate any leftovers in an airtight container or freeze for future use (see chart, page 12).

CHICKEN
CACCIATORE, 69

POULTRY

CASHEW CHICKEN

No need to order takeout when you can make rich and decadent cashew chicken at home. Cashews are added at the end of the cooking time so they retain a nice crunch. Serve this dish over a bed of white rice and garnish with sliced scallions for a punch of color and extra flavor. Grab your chopsticks, because this recipe is sure to be on repeat. Fortune cookies optional.

2 boneless, skinless chicken breasts, trimmed and cubed

2 tablespoons cornstarch

⅓ cup low-sodium soy sauce

¼ cup rice wine vinegar

¼ cup honey

3 or 4 garlic cloves, minced

½ teaspoon red pepper flakes

1 tablespoon ginger paste

1 cup roasted unsalted cashews

Serves **4**
Prep time: **15 minutes**
Cook time: **8 hours (Low)**
DAIRY-FREE

Tip: If you prefer the cashews softer, add them in step 1.

Per Serving (½ cup)
Calories: 372; Fat: 18g;
Protein: 24g;
Total Carbohydrates: 34g;
Fiber: 2g; Sugar: 20g;
Sodium: 802mg

1. In a large zip-top bag, combine the chicken and cornstarch. Seal the bag and shake to coat the chicken. Transfer the chicken to your slow cooker insert.

2. In a medium bowl, whisk the soy sauce, vinegar, honey, garlic, red pepper flakes, and ginger paste to combine. Pour the mixture over the chicken. Cover the cooker and cook on Low heat for 8 hours.

3. Stir in the cashews.

4. Refrigerate any leftovers in an airtight container or freeze for future use (see chart, page 12).

CHICKEN A L'ORANGE

Chicken a l'orange, or orange chicken, is a sweet and savory dish inspired by the iconic Julia Child. Chicken thighs are seasoned and then topped with an orange marmalade mixture. To complete the meal, serve the chicken with cauliflower gnocchi and garnish with sliced scallions. If the sauce isn't thick enough for your liking, stir in a sprinkle of cornstarch at the end.

4 bone-in chicken thighs, skin removed

1 teaspoon kosher salt, plus more for seasoning

¼ teaspoon freshly ground black pepper, plus more for seasoning

½ cup orange marmalade

2 cups Chicken Stock (page 125)

2 garlic cloves, minced

¼ cup low-sodium soy sauce

¼ cup honey

2 tablespoons champagne vinegar

Serves **4**
Prep time: **15 minutes**
Cook time: **8 hours (Low)**
DAIRY-FREE
NUT-FREE

Tips: Use kitchen shears to remove the chicken skin easily. Substitute white wine vinegar for the champagne vinegar, or clementine marmalade for the orange marmalade.

Per Serving (1 chicken thigh)
Calories: 346; Fat: 6g;
Protein: 30g;
Total Carbohydrates: 45g;
Fiber: 1g; Sugar: 40g;
Sodium: 1023mg

1. Season the chicken with the salt and pepper and place it in your slow cooker insert.

2. In a medium bowl, whisk the marmalade, chicken stock, garlic, soy sauce, honey, and vinegar to blend. Pour the orange sauce over the chicken. Cover the cooker and cook on Low heat for 8 hours. Taste and add more salt and pepper, as needed.

3. Refrigerate any leftovers in an airtight container or freeze for future use (see chart, page 12).

CHICKEN AND DUMPLINGS

Chicken and dumplings—or chicken 'n' dumplins, if you're from the South—is an American staple. It's also a very special dish to me. As a child I would ask my mom to make it for me and it would take her all day. She made everything from scratch, right down to the stock; there was love in every single bite. This recipe is my ode to her, with modifications to fit today's busy lifestyle.

4 boneless, skinless chicken thighs

2 teaspoons kosher salt, plus more for seasoning

½ teaspoon freshly ground black pepper, plus more for seasoning

2 tablespoons cornstarch

6 cups Chicken Stock (page 125)

2 garlic cloves, minced

1 onion, finely chopped

3 thyme sprigs

12 flat dumplings (preferably Anne's Old Fashioned brand)

Serves **4**
Prep time: **15 minutes**
Cook time: **8 hours, 15 minutes (Low)**
NUT-FREE

Tip: You can find Anne's Old Fashioned Flat Dumplings in the freezer section of select grocery stores, or online.

Per Serving (1 cup)
Calories: 304; Fat: 6g; Protein: 34g; Total Carbohydrates: 29g; Fiber: 0g; Sugar: 1g; Sodium: 717mg

1. Season the chicken with the salt and pepper and place it in a large zip-top bag. Add the cornstarch. Seal the bag and shake to coat the chicken. Transfer the chicken to your slow cooker insert.

2. Add the chicken stock, garlic, onion, and thyme. Cover the cooker and cook on Low heat for 8 hours. Taste and add more salt and pepper, as needed.

3. Add the dumplings to the cooker. Re-cover the cooker and cook for 10 to 15 minutes more or until the dumplings are cooked through.

4. Refrigerate any leftovers in an airtight container or freeze for future use (see chart, page 12).

CHICKEN CACCIATORE

Cacciatore means "hunter" in Italian. Chicken cacciatore is a hearty Italian stew made of chicken, tomatoes, mushrooms, and vegetables. It's comfort food best served over a bed of egg noodles with a handful of chopped fresh parsley sprinkled on top.

6 bone-in chicken thighs, skin removed

1 teaspoon kosher salt, plus more for seasoning

¼ teaspoon freshly ground black pepper, plus more for seasoning

1 garlic clove, minced

1 onion, finely chopped

2 carrots, finely chopped

2 celery stalks, trimmed and finely chopped

2 (14.5-ounce) cans diced tomatoes

⅔ cup white wine

8 ounces baby bella mushrooms, sliced

Serves **6**
Prep time: **15 minutes**
Cook time: **8 hours, 15 minutes (Low)**
DAIRY-FREE
NUT-FREE

Tip: Substitute chicken stock for the white wine, if you prefer.

Per Serving (1 thigh)
Calories: 303; Fat: 9g;
Protein: 41g;
Total Carbohydrates: 11g;
Fiber: 4g; Sugar: 6g;
Sodium: 557mg

1. Season the chicken with the salt and pepper and place it in your slow cooker insert.

2. Stir in the garlic, onion, carrots, celery, tomatoes with their juices, and white wine. Cover the cooker and cook on Low heat for 8 hours. Taste and add more salt and pepper, as needed.

3. Add the mushrooms to the cooker. Re-cover the pot and cook for 15 minutes more.

4. Refrigerate any leftovers in an airtight container or freeze for future use (see chart, page 12).

SALSA CHICKEN ENCHILADAS

This recipe uses two other recipes from this book, Salsa Chicken with Black Beans and Corn (page 83) and Enchilada Sauce (page 129). Corn tortillas are traditional with enchiladas, but they don't hold up as well in this casserole, so flour tortillas it is. If you would like to up the decadence, add more cheese to each enchilada before rolling. I like to top the enchiladas with sliced avocado, sour cream or Mexican crema, and chopped fresh cilantro.

Nonstick cooking spray

12 small flour tortillas

3 cups Salsa Chicken with Black Beans and Corn (page 83)

1 cup shredded Mexican cheese blend

4½ cups Enchilada Sauce (page 129)

2 cups water

Serves **6**
Prep time: **15 minutes**
Cook time: **8 hours (Low)**
NUT-FREE

Tip: If you have no leftover Enchilada Sauce (page 129) on hand, use your favorite store-bought sauce instead.

Per Serving (2 enchiladas)
Calories: 386; Fat: 11g;
Protein: 19g;
Total Carbohydrates: 54g;
Fiber: 8g; Sugar: 10g;
Sodium: 1497mg

1. Coat your slow cooker insert with cooking spray.

2. Place the tortillas on a work surface. Place ¼ cup of Salsa Chicken in the middle of each tortilla. Sprinkle each with a little cheese. Roll up the tortillas around the filling and place them, seam-side down, in a single layer in the prepared insert.

3. Pour the enchilada sauce and water over the enchiladas. Cover the cooker and cook on Low heat for 8 hours.

4. Top the enchiladas with the remaining cheese. Re-cover the cooker and cook for 1 to 2 minutes, just enough to melt the cheese.

5. Refrigerate any leftovers in an airtight container or freeze for future use (see chart, page 12).

CHICKEN MARSALA

Chicken Marsala is an Italian dish with chicken, mushrooms, and Marsala wine. It's so rich and luxurious that after one bite, you might imagine it would be fussy to make. However, when using a slow cooker, it practically prepares itself.

6 boneless, skinless chicken thighs

1 teaspoon kosher salt, plus more for seasoning

¼ teaspoon freshly ground black pepper, plus more for seasoning

⅓ cup all-purpose flour

1 tablespoon extra-virgin olive oil

1 onion, finely chopped

2 or 3 slices prosciutto, torn into pieces

1 cup Marsala wine

1½ cups Chicken Stock (page 125)

8 ounces white button mushrooms, sliced

Serves **6**
Prep time: **15 minutes**
Cook time: **8 hours (Low)**
DAIRY-FREE
NUT-FREE

Tips: If you opt for store-bought chicken stock, choose a low-sodium variety. You can also purchase pre-sliced mushrooms for convenience.

Per Serving (1 chicken thigh)
Calories: 342; Fat: 11g;
Protein: 41g;
Total Carbohydrates: 10g;
Fiber: 1g; Sugar: 2g;
Sodium: 487mg

1. In a large zip-top bag, combine the chicken, salt, pepper, and flour. Seal the bag and shake to coat the chicken.

2. In a heavy-bottomed pan over medium heat, heat the olive oil. Remove the chicken from the bag, shake off any excess flour, and add it to the pan. Cook the chicken on both sides until golden. Transfer the chicken to your slow cooker insert.

3. Add the onion and prosciutto to the pan. Sauté until softened. Stir in the Marsala, scraping up the browned bits from the bottom of the pan. Transfer the mixture to the slow cooker. Add the chicken stock and mushrooms. Cover the cooker and cook on Low heat for 8 hours.

4. Refrigerate any leftovers in an airtight container or freeze for future use (see chart, page 12).

CHICKEN POTPIE

Chicken potpie is the quintessential stick-to-your-ribs comfort food. This version can be finished a few different ways, depending on your time constraints and personal preferences. If biscuits aren't your cup of tea, cut a piece of puff pastry or piecrust into eight equal portions and bake them according to the package directions. Serve each pastry wedge atop a cup of potpie filling and garnish with chopped fresh parsley.

4 boneless, skinless chicken thighs

1 teaspoon kosher salt, plus more for seasoning

¼ teaspoon freshly ground black pepper, plus more for seasoning

½ cup all-purpose flour

1 tablespoon extra-virgin olive oil

1 onion, finely chopped

2 celery stalks, finely chopped

3 carrots, finely chopped

2 garlic cloves, minced

¼ cup Marsala wine

¼ teaspoon ground nutmeg

1 potato, peeled and chopped

2½ cups Chicken Stock (page 125)

1 tube store-bought uncooked biscuits (8 biscuits)

1 cup heavy (whipping) cream

1 cup frozen peas

Serves **8**
Prep time: **15 minutes**
Cook time: **8 hours, 10 minutes (Low)**
NUT-FREE

Per Serving (1 cup)
Calories: 448; Fat: 21g;
Protein: 24g;
Total Carbohydrates: 39g;
Fiber: 3g; Sugar: 4g;
Sodium: 502mg

1. Season the chicken with the salt and pepper and place it in a large zip-top bag. Add the flour. Seal the bag and shake to coat the chicken.

2. In a heavy-bottomed pan over medium heat, heat the olive oil. Remove the chicken from the bag, shake off any excess flour, and add it to the pan. Cook the chicken on both sides until golden. Transfer the chicken to your slow cooker insert.

3. Add the onion, celery, carrots, and garlic to the pan. Sauté until just softened. Stir in the Marsala, scraping up the browned bits from the bottom of the pan to deglaze it. Transfer the mixture to your slow cooker insert.

4. Stir in the nutmeg, potato, and chicken stock. Cover the cooker and cook on Low heat for 8 hours. Taste and add more salt and pepper, as needed.

5. While the chicken cooks, prepare the biscuits according to the package directions.

6. Stir in the heavy cream and peas. Re-cover the cooker and cook for 5 to 10 minutes. Serve the chicken potpie with the biscuits.

7. Refrigerate any leftovers in an airtight container or freeze for future use (see chart, page 12).

CHICKEN ROPA VIEJA

Ropa vieja is a Cuban dish, typically made with skirt steak. This version is inspired by that traditional rendition but uses chicken for a more budget-friendly meal. Leftovers are equally delicious, making for a great next-day lunch. Serve this chicken over plain white rice, or make a fun bowl with rice, beans, and shredded cheese.

3 boneless, skinless chicken thighs

1 (14.5-ounce) can diced tomatoes

2 bell peppers, any color, seeded and cut into strips

1 onion, finely chopped

2 tablespoons diced fresh tomato

Juice of 1 lime

1 teaspoon kosher salt, plus more for seasoning

1 garlic clove, minced

1 teaspoon ground cumin

Serves **6**
Prep time: **15 minutes**
Cook time: **8 hours (Low)**
DAIRY-FREE
NUT-FREE

Per Serving (½ cup)
Calories: 193; Fat: 5g;
Protein: 22g;
Total Carbohydrates: 17g;
Fiber: 8g; Sugar: 11g;
Sodium: 564mg

1. In your slow cooker insert, stir together the chicken, tomatoes with their juices, bell peppers, onion, fresh tomato, lime juice, salt, garlic, and cumin. Cover the cooker and cook on Low heat for 8 hours. Taste and add more salt, as needed.

2. Refrigerate any leftovers in an airtight container or freeze for future use (see chart, page 12).

BARBECUE CHICKEN

As a Southerner at heart, I enjoy everything barbecue, but especially barbecue chicken. After slow cooking, the chicken can be cut into pieces and enjoyed whole, or it can be shredded and used in sandwiches, nachos, or even as a pizza topping, depending on what you're craving. Whichever route you go, don't forget a side of coleslaw.

Nonstick cooking spray

1 (5-pound) whole chicken

1 teaspoon kosher salt

½ teaspoon freshly ground black pepper

1 onion, halved

1½ cups Barbecue Sauce (page 128)

Serves **8**
Prep time: **5 minutes**
Cook time: **8 hours (Low)**
NUT-FREE

Tip: Substitute your favorite store-bought barbecue sauce, if you prefer. I like Sweet Baby Ray's brand.

Per Serving
Calories: 312; Fat: 14g;
Protein: 30g;
Total Carbohydrates: 16g;
Fiber: 0g; Sugar: 13g;
Sodium: 386mg

1. Coat your slow cooker insert with cooking spray.

2. Pat the chicken dry. Remove any gizzards from the chicken's cavity. Season the chicken all over with the salt and pepper. Put the onion in the chicken cavity and transfer the chicken to the prepared slow cooker insert.

3. Pour the barbecue sauce over the chicken, making sure it is completely coated. Cover the cooker and cook on Low heat for 8 hours.

4. Refrigerate any leftovers in an airtight container or freeze for future use (see chart, page 12).

CLASSIC WHOLE CHICKEN

Trust me, a whole chicken is a beautiful thing. It can be turned into multiple meals and the flavor possibilities are almost endless. Here, I season the chicken simply with herb butter, which is rubbed both under and over the skin. If you want to crisp the skin, transfer the cooked chicken to an oven-safe dish and place it under the broiler just until crisped.

1 (5-pound) whole chicken

1 small onion

½ lemon

6 tablespoons (¾ stick) unsalted butter, at room temperature

1 tablespoon kosher salt

2 teaspoons freshly ground black pepper

1 teaspoon garlic powder

1 teaspoon Italian seasoning

Serves **8**
Prep time: **15 minutes**
Cook time: **8 hours (Low)**
NUT-FREE

Tips: Check to make sure all gizzards are removed from the chicken's cavity before starting to prepare this recipe. Also, save those chicken bones to make Chicken Stock (page 125) or Chicken Broth (page 124).

Per Serving
Calories: 326; Fat: 22g;
Protein: 29g;
Total Carbohydrates: 1g;
Fiber: 0g; Sugar: 0g;
Sodium: 236mg

1. Pat the chicken dry with paper towels. Place the onion and lemon half inside the chicken cavity.

2. In a small bowl, mix together the butter, salt, pepper, garlic powder, and Italian seasoning.

3. Using a small paring knife, carefully cut the membrane where the chicken skin is attached to the meat. This will allow you to insert the butter under the skin more easily. Carefully spoon half the butter mixture underneath the chicken skin. Massage the butter down as far as you can go without tearing the skin. Rub the remaining butter mixture over the outside of the chicken. Transfer to your slow cooker insert. Cover and cook on Low heat for 8 hours.

4. Remove the chicken from the cooker and discard the onion and lemon half. Slice and serve.

5. Refrigerate any leftovers in an airtight container or freeze for future use (see chart, page 12).

CORNISH HENS

Cornish hens—also called Cornish rock game hens—weigh no more than 2 pounds apiece. They're wonderful for a special-occasion dinner but are also effortless enough for a weeknight meal. Seasoned and paired with carrots and onion, they're slow-cooked until tender. If you would like to crisp the skin, transfer the cooked hens to an oven-safe dish and place under the broiler just until crisped. Serve the hens with a side of wild rice.

2 Cornish game hens

2 teaspoons Italian seasoning

1 teaspoon kosher salt

1 pound baby carrots

½ onion, chopped

Serves **4**
Prep time: **15 minutes**
Cook time: **8 hours (Low)**
DAIRY-FREE
NUT-FREE

1. Pat the game hens dry using a paper towel. Season them all over with the Italian seasoning and salt. Place the hens in your slow cooker insert.

2. Place the carrots and onion around the hens. Cover the cooker and cook on Low heat for 8 hours.

3. Refrigerate any leftovers in an airtight container or freeze for future use (see chart, page 12).

Tip: Substitute 3 regular carrots, cut into 2-inch sections, for the baby carrots.

Per Serving (½ hen)
Calories: 388; Fat: 24g;
Protein: 30g;
Total Carbohydrates: 12g;
Fiber: 3g; Sugar: 6g;
Sodium: 472mg

CREAMY CHICKEN THIGHS WITH SPINACH AND ARTICHOKES

If you're a fan of spinach and artichoke dip, this chicken dish will be right up your alley. Chicken thighs are cooked with marinated jarred artichokes; there's no need to drain the marinade, as it brings great flavor. You'll finish the dish with cream, cheese, and fresh spinach, cooking for just long enough to wilt the spinach and warm the cream. Serve this dish over cooked pasta or gnocchi.

4 boneless, skinless chicken thighs

1 teaspoon kosher salt, plus more for seasoning

1 (12-ounce) jar quartered marinated artichokes

2 garlic cloves, minced

1 cup Chicken Stock (page 125)

½ cup heavy (whipping) cream

¾ cup grated Parmesan cheese

4 ounces fresh spinach

Serves **4**
Prep time: **15 minutes**
Cook time: **8 hours (Low)**
NUT-FREE

Tips: Save the chicken bones to make Chicken Stock (page 125) or Chicken Broth (page 124). Substitute half-and-half for the heavy cream for a lighter meal.

Per Serving (1 thigh)
Calories: 527; Fat: 31g;
Protein: 47g;
Total Carbohydrates: 14g;
Fiber: 7g; Sugar: 2g;
Sodium: 893mg

1. Place the chicken in your slow cooker insert. Season it with the salt and top with the artichokes and their marinade, the garlic, and chicken stock. Cover the cooker and cook on Low heat for 8 hours.

2. Stir in the heavy cream and Parmesan. Add the spinach. Re-cover the cooker and cook just until the spinach is wilted, 1 to 2 minutes. Taste and add more salt, as needed.

3. Refrigerate any leftovers in an airtight container or freeze for future use (see chart, page 12).

CHICKEN WITH 40 CLOVES OF GARLIC

Chicken with 40 cloves of garlic is a classic French dish. Yes, there really are 40 cloves of garlic in here. If that sounds like a lot, it is. However, as the dish cooks, the garlic mellows and helps create the beautiful sauce that accompanies the chicken. I like to serve this chicken over rice or pasta and garnish with a sprinkling of chopped fresh parsley. You may even want to grab a baguette and spread a few of the cooked garlic cloves on some slices. It's divine.

6 bone-in chicken thighs, skin removed

¼ cup all-purpose flour

1 teaspoon kosher salt, plus more for seasoning

½ teaspoon freshly ground black pepper, plus more for seasoning

40 garlic cloves (about 3 heads), peeled

1 cup Chicken Stock (page 125)

½ cup white wine, such as pinot grigio

2 tablespoons unsalted butter

Juice of 1 lemon

Serves **6**
Prep time: **15 minutes**
Cook time: **8 hours (Low)**
NUT-FREE

Tip: Purchase pre-peeled garlic cloves to save prep time.

Per Serving (1 thigh)
Calories: 312; Fat: 12g;
Protein: 39g;
Total Carbohydrates: 7g;
Fiber: 0g; Sugar: 0g;
Sodium: 379mg

1. In a large zip-top bag, combine the chicken, flour, salt, and pepper. Seal the bag and shake to coat the chicken. Transfer the chicken to your slow cooker insert. Discard any excess flour.

2. Add the garlic, chicken stock, white wine, and butter to the cooker. Cover the cooker and cook on Low heat for 8 hours. Taste and add more salt and pepper, as needed.

3. Pour the lemon juice into the slow cooker insert and stir to combine.

4. Refrigerate any leftovers in an airtight container or freeze for future use (see chart, page 12).

BUTTER CHICKEN

In some recipes, the sauce is the star. This is one of those recipes. I get lost in this sumptuous sauce every single time. It's tangy, mild, and rich with tomato. It also happens to involve a full stick of butter. Sign me up. Serve this chicken over rice or with naan to enhance the richness. If you're "team cilantro," like me, add a heaping handful to garnish.

2 boneless, skinless chicken breasts

2 (8-ounce) cans tomato sauce

1 cup Chicken Stock (page 125)

½ onion, finely chopped

2 tablespoons garam masala

1 teaspoon ground cumin

1 teaspoon ground turmeric

1 teaspoon ground ginger

1 teaspoon kosher salt

½ teaspoon freshly ground black pepper

¼ teaspoon cayenne pepper

8 tablespoons (1 stick) unsalted butter

1 cup heavy (whipping) cream

Serves **6**
Prep time: **15 minutes**
Cook time: **8 hours (Low)**
NUT-FREE

Tips: Substitute 4 boneless, skinless chicken thighs for the chicken breasts. You may also substitute Vegetable Broth (page 127) for the chicken stock.

Per Serving (1 cup)
Calories: 366; Fat: 32g;
Protein: 13g;
Total Carbohydrates: 10g;
Fiber: 2g; Sugar: 5g;
Sodium: 255mg

1. In your slow cooker insert, stir together the chicken, tomato sauce, chicken stock, onion, garam masala, cumin, turmeric, ginger, salt, black pepper, cayenne, and butter. Cover the cooker and cook on Low heat for 8 hours.

2. Transfer the chicken to a work surface and cut it into cubes. Return the chicken to the cooker and stir it into the sauce.

3. Stir in the cream.

4. Refrigerate any leftovers in an airtight container or freeze for future use (see chart, page 12).

LEMON BUTTER CHICKEN

Lemon butter chicken is fresh and full of zest with a bright sauce just begging to be served with pasta. Angel hair pasta works well here. I recommend removing the chicken breasts and cutting them before serving. Add the cooked pasta to the slow cooker insert and toss to coat in the sauce, then plate the chicken slices on top of the pasta. Garnish with chopped fresh parsley and lemon slices, if desired.

3 boneless, skinless chicken breasts, fat trimmed

3 garlic cloves, crushed

2 tablespoons unsalted butter

1½ cups Chicken Stock (page 125)

1½ cups dry white wine

Zest and juice of 1 lemon

1 teaspoon kosher salt, plus more for seasoning

½ teaspoon Italian seasoning

¼ teaspoon freshly ground black pepper, plus more for seasoning

Serves **6**
Prep time: **15 minutes**
Cook time: **8 hours (Low)**
NUT-FREE

Tip: Zest the lemon before juicing it.

Per Serving (½ chicken breast)
Calories: 171; Fat: 6g;
Protein: 16g;
Total Carbohydrates: 3g;
Fiber: 0g; Sugar: 0g;
Sodium: 227mg

1. In your slow cooker insert, stir together the chicken, garlic, butter, chicken stock, white wine, lemon zest, lemon juice, salt, Italian seasoning, and pepper. Cover the cooker and cook on Low heat for 8 hours. Taste and add more salt and pepper, as needed.

2. Refrigerate any leftovers in an airtight container or freeze for future use (see chart, page 12).

PESTO CHICKEN

Pesto, which comes in many varieties, is very versatile. Use a traditional pesto or try this recipe with a kale or sun-dried tomato version. Or get creative and make your own! In this recipe the chicken cooks in a mixture of pesto and stock for maximum flavor and tenderness. I like to finish this dish by adding cooked pasta or even gnocchi. Garnish with a grating of fresh Parmesan, if you're feeling fancy.

Nonstick cooking spray

4 boneless, skinless chicken thighs

1 teaspoon kosher salt, plus more for seasoning

¼ teaspoon freshly ground black pepper, plus more for seasoning

1 (6.7-ounce) jar pesto (I like Priano brand)

2 cups Chicken Stock (page 125)

Serves **4**
Prep time: **15 minutes**
Cook time: **8 hours (Low)**

Tip: Once you've emptied the pesto jar, pour a little chicken stock into it. Seal and shake to get any remaining pesto out.

Per Serving (1 chicken thigh)
Calories: 443; Fat: 34g;
Protein: 32g;
Total Carbohydrates: 2g;
Fiber: 1g; Sugar: 0g;
Sodium: 782mg

1. Coat your slow cooker insert with cooking spray.

2. Season the chicken with the salt and pepper and place it in the prepared insert.

3. In a medium bowl, whisk the pesto and chicken stock to blend. Pour the sauce over the chicken. Cover the cooker and cook on Low heat for 8 hours. Taste and add more salt and pepper, as needed.

4. Refrigerate any leftovers in an airtight container or freeze for future use (see chart, page 12).

SALSA CHICKEN WITH BLACK BEANS AND CORN

Don't be surprised if this recipe becomes a new family favorite. You'll love that it's extremely versatile and typically makes enough for a second meal. The salsa choice is yours; if you like it spicy, go for it. This is truly a load-and-go recipe. Enjoy this dish as is or turn it into Salsa Chicken Enchiladas (page 70), quesadillas, or even nachos.

2 large boneless, skinless chicken breasts

1 (16-ounce) jar thick, chunky salsa

1 (15.25-ounce) can corn kernels, drained

1 (15.5-ounce) can black beans, drained and rinsed

Serves **6 to 8**
Prep time: **5 minutes**
Cook time: **8 hours (Low)**
DAIRY-FREE
NUT-FREE

Tip: Garnish with shredded Mexican cheese blend, chopped fresh cilantro, and avocado slices, if desired.

Per Serving (1 cup)
Calories: 178; Fat: 2g;
Protein: 16g;
Total Carbohydrates: 26g;
Fiber: 8g; Sugar: 6g;
Sodium: 701mg

1. In your slow cooker insert, stir together the chicken, salsa, corn, and black beans, making sure the chicken is covered with the salsa. Cover the cooker and cook on Low heat for 8 hours.

2. Remove the chicken and, using two forks, shred it. Return the chicken to the cooker and stir to combine.

3. Refrigerate any leftovers in an airtight container or freeze for future use (see chart, page 12).

SALSA VERDE CHICKEN LEGS

Salsa verde translates to "green sauce." True to its name, the sauce is indeed green, thanks to its base of tomatillos. It's tangy, zesty, and makes a great dip, topping, or—as in this case—base for a sauce for tender chicken.

6 chicken legs, skin removed

1 teaspoon kosher salt

¼ teaspoon freshly ground black pepper

1 (17.6-ounce) jar salsa verde (I like Goya brand)

1 cup Chicken Stock (page 125)

Serves **6**

Prep time: **15 minutes**

Cook time: **8 hours (Low)**

DAIRY-FREE

NUT-FREE

Tip: Use kitchen shears to easily remove the chicken skin.

Per Serving (1 chicken leg)
Calories: 351; Fat: 12g;
Protein: 51g;
Total Carbohydrates: 6g;
Fiber: 2g; Sugar: 3g;
Sodium: 876mg

1. Season the chicken with the salt and pepper and put it in your slow cooker insert.

2. Stir in the salsa and chicken stock to combine. Cover the cooker and cook on Low heat for 8 hours.

3. Refrigerate any leftovers in an airtight container or freeze for future use (see chart, page 12).

SHREDDED BUFFALO CHICKEN

If you like a little kick to your chicken, buffalo chicken is most definitely for you. Although buffalo chicken is typically associated with wings, it is equally delicious when turned into other meals. Why not try buffalo chicken sliders, pizza, nachos, or baked potatoes? Whatever you decide, don't forget the extra napkins!

3 boneless, skinless chicken breasts, fat trimmed

16 ounces buffalo wing sauce, divided (I like Sweet Baby Ray's brand)

2 tablespoons unsalted butter

½ cup Chicken Stock (page 125)

Serves **8**
Prep time: **15 minutes**
Cook time: **8 hours (Low)**
NUT-FREE

Per Serving (½ cup)
Calories: 192; Fat: 4g;
Protein: 12g;
Total Carbohydrates: 26g;
Fiber: 1g; Sugar: 22g;
Sodium: 461mg

1. Put the chicken in your slow cooker insert. Pour three-fourths of the buffalo sauce over the chicken.

2. Add the butter and chicken stock. Cover the cooker and cook on Low heat for 8 hours.

3. Using two forks, shred the chicken in the slow cooker. Stir in the remaining buffalo sauce.

4. Refrigerate any leftovers in an airtight container or freeze for future use (see chart, page 12).

SHREDDED CHICKEN TACOS

These chicken tacos are as delicious as they are budget friendly. The chicken is seasoned with taco seasoning (super easy!) and gets an additional kick with a festive mango-peach salsa. If you have leftovers, turn the shredded chicken into nachos. And if you're feeling extra, top your tacos with shredded cheese, chopped fresh cilantro, additional salsa, and even a squeeze of lime juice. Margaritas are up to you.

1 tablespoon
taco seasoning

4 boneless, skinless
chicken thighs

3 garlic cloves, minced

1 (16-ounce) jar
mango-peach salsa

½ cup Chicken Stock
(page 125)

Juice of 1 lime

12 flour tortillas, or corn
tortillas, warmed

Serves **6**
Prep time: **15 minutes**
Cook time: **8 hours (Low)**
DAIRY-FREE
NUT-FREE

Tip: Substitute your favorite salsa in place of the mango-peach salsa.

Per Serving (2 tacos)
Calories: 362; Fat: 9g;
Protein: 31g;
Total Carbohydrates: 37g;
Fiber: 3g; Sugar: 5g;
Sodium: 934mg

1. Sprinkle the taco seasoning over both sides of the chicken and put the seasoned chicken in your slow cooker insert. Add the garlic, salsa, chicken stock, and lime juice. Cover the cooker and cook on Low heat for 8 hours.

2. Using two forks, shred the chicken in the slow cooker. Equally divide the shredded chicken among the tortillas to serve.

3. Refrigerate any leftovers in an airtight container or freeze for future use (see chart, page 12).

TURKEY MEATBALLS

If you're looking for a lighter meatball, look no further than turkey meatballs. Lean ground turkey is mixed with spices, such as allspice and nutmeg, as well as onion and garlic powder to pack a flavorful punch. Pack your meatballs well in the cookie scoop, so they retain their shape when cooking. Swap in your favorite store-bought marinara if you don't have time to make your own. Serve these meatballs over spaghetti or zoodles.

Nonstick cooking spray

1 pound ground turkey

½ cup panko
bread crumbs

½ cup whole milk

1 large egg, beaten

1 teaspoon kosher salt

½ teaspoon onion powder

½ teaspoon garlic powder

¼ teaspoon
ground allspice

¼ teaspoon
ground nutmeg

3 cups Marinara Sauce
(page 130)

Serves **8**
Prep time: **15 minutes**
Cook time: **8 hours (Low)**
NUT-FREE

Tip: Substitute traditional bread crumbs for the panko bread crumbs.

Per Serving (2 meatballs)
Calories: 261; Fat: 13g;
Protein: 27g;
Total Carbohydrates: 12g;
Fiber: 1g; Sugar: 6g;
Sodium: 678mg

1. Coat your slow cooker insert with the cooking spray.

2. In a large bowl, mix the ground turkey, panko, milk, egg, salt, onion powder, garlic powder, allspice, and nutmeg to combine. Using a large cookie scoop, scoop out 16 packed meatballs and place them in the prepared slow cooker insert, stacking the meatballs if necessary.

3. Pour the marinara sauce over the meatballs, making sure all the meatballs are coated. Cover the cooker and cook on Low heat for 8 hours.

4. Refrigerate any leftovers in an airtight container or freeze for future use (see chart, page 12).

CHICKEN TIKKA MASALA

Chicken cooked slowly with spices, yogurt, and coconut milk creates a vibrant, flavorful dish that you'll be craving often. This dish provides incredible flavor without the heat, but add some cayenne for a kick if you like. I prefer this on the saucier side, so I use just two chicken thighs. Extra sauce means the dish is perfect to serve over a bed of jasmine rice or with a side of naan. A garnish of chopped fresh cilantro brightens the presentation.

2 boneless, skinless chicken thighs

1 (13.5-ounce) can coconut milk (shake before opening)

1 (5.3-ounce) container plain yogurt

1 (14.5-ounce) can fire-roasted diced tomatoes, drained

2 tablespoons tomato paste

1 tablespoon garam masala

1 tablespoon ginger paste

1 teaspoon kosher salt

1 teaspoon ground turmeric

½ teaspoon ground cumin

Chopped fresh cilantro, for garnish

Serves **4**
Prep time: **15 minutes**
Cook time: **8 hours (Low)**

Tip: Use a tablespoon measure to scoop any remaining tomato paste from the can and freeze it in portions for future use.

Per Serving (1 cup)
Calories: 354; Fat: 25g;
Protein: 24g;
Total Carbohydrates: 11g;
Fiber: 3g; Sugar: 6g;
Sodium: 535mg

1. In your slow cooker insert, stir together the chicken, coconut milk, yogurt, tomatoes, tomato paste, garam masala, ginger paste, salt, turmeric, and cumin. Cover the cooker and cook on Low heat for 8 hours. Garnish with cilantro to serve.

2. Refrigerate any leftovers in an airtight container or freeze for future use (see chart, page 12).

GINGER-SOY PULLED PORK, 105

BEEF, PORK, AND LAMB

BABY BACK RIBS

Baby back ribs are known for being fall-off-the-bone tender. That does not happen quickly, so cooking them in a slow cooker is a fantastic way to achieve the desired results. Don't skip removing the membrane, or silver skin, from the back of the ribs, so the ribs absorb as much flavor as possible. My all-purpose rub mixture is always crowd-pleasing; it's great on other proteins as well. These ribs can be served as is or slathered in your favorite barbecue sauce.

2 tablespoons kosher salt

2 tablespoons packed light brown sugar

1 teaspoon chili powder

1 teaspoon garlic powder

1 teaspoon red pepper flakes

1 (3½-pound) rack baby back ribs, membrane removed (see Tip), rack quartered

1 cup beer

Serves **4**
Prep time: **15 minutes**
Cook time: **8 hours (Low)**
DAIRY-FREE
NUT-FREE

Tip: To remove the membrane from the backside of the ribs, run a knife down the middle and grab the membrane with a paper towel. Pull off the membrane and discard it.

Per Serving (2 to 3 ribs)
Calories: 362; Fat: 23g;
Protein: 25g;
Total Carbohydrates: 10g;
Fiber: 0g; Sugar: 7g;
Sodium: 1799mg

1. In a small bowl, stir together the salt, brown sugar, chili powder, garlic powder, and red pepper flakes. Rub the spice mixture over the ribs, then put them in your slow cooker insert.

2. Pour the beer around the ribs, not on top, to avoid washing off the spice rub. Cover the cooker and cook on Low heat for 8 hours. Discard the cooking liquid and serve.

3. Refrigerate any leftovers in an airtight container or freeze for future use (see chart, page 12).

BALSAMIC-BRAISED SHORT RIBS

Don't let the name fool you: Short ribs are not short on flavor. Once you've seasoned the ribs, they need to be browned to produce that delicious savory flavor. When they're ready to turn, the meat will release naturally from the bottom of the pan; if they cling to the pan, wait a bit. I like to serve my short ribs over a bed of parsnip puree, but they're equally delicious over mashed potatoes, polenta, or even pasta.

2 pounds beef short ribs, cut into individual ribs

1 teaspoon kosher salt, plus more for seasoning

¼ teaspoon freshly ground black pepper, plus more for seasoning

1 teaspoon Italian seasoning

1 tablespoon extra-virgin olive oil

2 cups Beef Stock (page 123)

1 cup red wine, such as merlot

¼ cup balsamic vinegar

1 tablespoon Dijon mustard

1 tablespoon packed light brown sugar

2 or 3 thyme sprigs

Serves **4**
Prep time: **15 minutes**
Cook time: **8 hours (Low)**
DAIRY-FREE
NUT-FREE

Tips: If you have time, take the ribs out of the refrigerator 30 minutes before cooking for better browning. Be sure to save your leftover bones to make Beef Stock (page 123) or Beef Broth (page 122).

Per Serving (1 short rib)
Calories: 608; Fat: 44g;
Protein: 40g;
Total Carbohydrates: 8g;
Fiber: 0g; Sugar: 6g;
Sodium: 541mg

1. Season the ribs all over with the salt, pepper, and Italian seasoning.

2. In a heavy-bottomed pan over medium heat, heat the olive oil. Add the ribs and cook, turning, until they're browned on all sides. Transfer the ribs to your slow cooker insert.

3. Combine the beef stock, red wine, vinegar, mustard, and brown sugar and add to the ribs. Place the thyme on top. Cover the cooker and cook on Low heat for 8 hours. Taste and add more salt and pepper, as needed.

4. Refrigerate any leftovers in an airtight container or freeze for future use (see chart, page 12).

BALSAMIC-DIJON POT ROAST

Pot roast is a classic meal that has been popular with families for generations. Chuck roast is the go-to cut of beef because it stands up to slow cooking all day, emerging perfectly fork-tender. This isn't your typical pot roast, though; it's flavored with balsamic vinegar and Dijon mustard to give it a little something special. Serve this roast with a side of steamed new potatoes to sop up that gorgeous gravy.

1 (2-pound) beef chuck roast

1 teaspoon kosher salt, plus more for seasoning

½ teaspoon freshly ground black pepper

1 onion, finely chopped

4 to 6 carrots, cut into 2-inch pieces

⅓ cup balsamic vinegar

3 cups Beef Stock (page 123)

2 tablespoons Dijon mustard

Serves **10**
Prep time: **15 minutes**
Cook time: **8 hours (Low)**
DAIRY-FREE
NUT-FREE

Tip: If the sauce is too thin, thicken it with a cornstarch or arrowroot powder slurry: In a small bowl, whisk 1 tablespoon of cornstarch or arrowroot with about ½ cup of liquid from the slow cooker until dissolved. Stir the slurry into the slow cooker and let the sauce thicken.

Per Serving (1 cup)
Calories: 181; Fat: 10g;
Protein: 18g;
Total Carbohydrates: 5g;
Fiber: 1g; Sugar: 3g;
Sodium: 244mg

1. Season the roast all over with the salt and pepper and put it in your slow cooker insert.

2. Arrange the onion and carrots around the roast.

3. In a medium bowl, whisk the vinegar, beef stock, and mustard to blend. Pour the sauce over the roast. Cover the cooker and cook on Low heat for 8 hours. Taste and season with more salt and pepper, as needed.

4. Using two forks, shred the roast in the slow cooker and mix it with the sauce and vegetables.

5. Refrigerate any leftovers in an airtight container or freeze for future use (see chart, page 12).

BEEF STROGANOFF

Beef stroganoff originated in Russia and is made using a very inexpensive cut of beef, such as stew meat. The dish is rich, comforting, and creamy thanks to the sour cream, which is stirred in at the end. Beef stroganoff is typically served over egg noodles or rice, which you could make the night before for convenience and simply reheat. You can even add sliced mushrooms to the slow cooker, too, if you like.

1½ pounds beef stew meat

2 cups Beef Stock (page 123)

3 tablespoons Worcestershire sauce

2 tablespoons Dijon mustard

1 teaspoon kosher salt, plus more for seasoning

½ teaspoon freshly ground black pepper, plus more for seasoning

½ teaspoon garlic powder

½ teaspoon onion powder

½ cup sour cream

Serves **6**
Prep time: **15 minutes**
Cook time: **8 hours (Low)**
NUT-FREE

Tip: Substitute cream cheese, at room temperature, for the sour cream.

Per Serving (½ cup)
Calories: 188; Fat: 8g;
Protein: 25g;
Total Carbohydrates: 3g;
Fiber: 0g; Sugar: 1g;
Sodium: 435mg

1. In your slow cooker insert, stir together the beef, beef stock, Worcestershire sauce, mustard, salt, pepper, garlic powder, and onion powder. Cover the cooker and cook on Low heat for 8 hours. Taste and add more salt and pepper, as needed.

2. Stir in the sour cream before serving.

3. Refrigerate any leftovers in an airtight container or freeze for future use (see chart, page 12).

BEER BRATS

Popular in the Midwest, beer brats are bratwursts that have been seared then cooked in beer with onions. Although they're perfect for tailgating and family picnics, I think they're great any time the craving hits. To get a uniform slice on the onions and to cut them quickly, I use a mandoline. I also like to toast the rolls. If you'd like, add sauerkraut and a smattering of dry mustard.

2 pounds brats

1 large onion, sliced

2 (12-ounce) cans light beer

2 tablespoons Dijon mustard

2 tablespoons unsalted butter

1 teaspoon hot sauce

6 potato rolls, split

Serves **6**
Prep time: **15 minutes**
Cook time: **8 hours (Low)**
NUT-FREE

Tip: Slice the onion the night before for convenience when assembling the next day.

Per Serving (1 brat with bun and onion)
Calories: 590; Fat: 38g;
Protein: 21g;
Total Carbohydrates: 31g;
Fiber: 2g; Sugar: 4g;
Sodium: 1239mg

1. Heat a grill pan or skillet over medium heat and sear the brats on both sides until grill marks appear. Transfer the brats to your slow cooker insert.

2. Stir in the onion, beer, mustard, butter, and hot sauce. Cover the cooker and cook on Low heat for 8 hours.

3. To assemble, place 1 brat in each roll and top with some of the cooked onion.

4. Refrigerate any leftovers in an airtight container or freeze for future use (see chart, page 12).

BONELESS VEAL ROAST

Roasts are usually associated with Sunday supper, but because we're cooking this beauty in the slow cooker, it's easy to enjoy it any day of the week. If you want to add a starch, a microwave steamer bag of new potatoes would be a quick and easy side.

1 (2-pound) boneless veal chuck roast

2 teaspoons kosher salt, plus more for seasoning

½ teaspoon freshly ground black pepper, plus more for seasoning

2 tablespoons extra-virgin olive oil

1 onion, finely chopped

2 celery stalks, finely chopped

2 carrots, finely chopped

1 cup dry white wine

1 (14.5-ounce) can diced tomatoes

Serves **6**
Prep time: **15 minutes**
Cook time: **8 hours (Low)**
DAIRY-FREE
NUT-FREE

Tip: Prepare the vegetables the night before for convenience when assembling.

Per Serving (½ cup)
Calories: 299; Fat: 13g;
Protein: 32g;
Total Carbohydrates: 7g;
Fiber: 2g; Sugar: 4g;
Sodium: 617mg

1. Season the roast all over with the salt and pepper.

2. In a large heavy-bottomed pan over medium heat, heat the olive oil. Add the roast and cook until it is evenly browned on all sides. Transfer the roast to your slow cooker insert.

3. To the hot pan, add the onion, celery, and carrots. Sauté until just softened.

4. Stir the white wine into the pan, scraping up the browned bits from the bottom of the pan to deglaze it. Transfer the mixture to the slow cooker insert.

5. Stir in the tomatoes with their juices. Cover the cooker and cook on Low heat for 8 hours. Taste and add more salt and pepper, as needed.

6. Refrigerate any leftovers in an airtight container or freeze for future use (see chart, page 12).

BRISKET TACOS

My best friend from Dallas told me about Dallas-style brisket tacos and now I'm not sure I can live without them. Beef brisket is seasoned and quickly browned, then slow-cooked the rest of the way. The remaining ingredients don't need much attention because they'll be strained at the end, making this a super convenient recipe for your slow cooker. Once shredded, the beef goes great with flour tortillas and a dollop of salsa.

1 (2½-pound) beef brisket

1 tablespoon kosher salt

½ teaspoon freshly ground black pepper

2 tablespoons extra-virgin olive oil

1 onion, quartered

8 garlic cloves, peeled and crushed

1 jalapeño pepper, cut in half, seeded, and ribbed

1½ cups Beef Stock (page 123)

½ cup apple cider vinegar

12 flour tortillas

Serves **6**
Prep time: **15 minutes**
Cook time: **8 hours (Low)**
DAIRY-FREE
NUT-FREE

Per Serving (2 tacos)
Calories: 439; Fat: 20g;
Protein: 42g;
Total Carbohydrates: 19g;
Fiber: 1g; Sugar: 2g;
Sodium: 946mg

1. Season the brisket all over with the salt and pepper.

2. In a large heavy-bottomed pan over medium-high heat, heat the olive oil. Add the brisket and cook until it is evenly browned on both sides. Transfer the brisket to your slow cooker insert.

3. Arrange the onion, garlic, and jalapeño around the brisket. Pour the stock and vinegar on top. Cover the cooker and cook on Low heat for 8 hours.

4. Transfer the brisket to a work surface and, using two forks, shred it.

5. Place a fine-mesh sieve over a medium heat-proof bowl and strain the liquid from the cooker into the bowl. Return the strained liquid and shredded brisket to the slow cooker insert. Discard the onion, garlic, and jalapeño.

6. Top the flour tortillas with the brisket and sauce and serve.

7. Refrigerate any leftovers in an airtight container or freeze for future use (see chart, page 12).

CHICKEN AND SAUSAGE JAMBALAYA

Jambalaya is a favorite New Orleans dish that's big on flavor. This recipe uses budget-friendly boneless, skinless chicken thighs and smoked sausage. You can substitute smoked andouille sausage, if you prefer. Mix the cooked rice in at the end; the amount to use will depend on how you like your jambalaya. I suggest a garnish of chopped fresh parsley to finish.

4 boneless, skinless chicken thighs, cubed

10 ounces smoked sausage, cut into 1-inch pieces

2 (14.5-ounce) cans diced tomatoes, drained

1 onion, finely chopped

1 celery stalk, finely chopped

2 cups Chicken Stock (page 125)

2 garlic cloves, minced

1 tablespoon Creole seasoning (I like Tony Chachere's brand)

1 to 2 cups cooked rice

Serves **8**
Prep time: **15 minutes**
Cook time: **8 hours (Low)**
DAIRY-FREE
NUT-FREE

Tip: Prepare the vegetables and cook the rice the night before for convenience during assembly.

Per Serving (1 cup)
Calories: 251; Fat: 14g;
Protein: 20g;
Total Carbohydrates: 12g;
Fiber: 3g; Sugar: 3g;
Sodium: 519mg

1. In your slow cooker insert, stir together the chicken, sausage, tomatoes, onion, celery, chicken stock, garlic, and seasoning. Cover the cooker and cook on Low heat for 8 hours.

2. Stir in the rice before serving.

3. Refrigerate any leftovers in an airtight container or freeze for future use (see chart, page 12).

CLASSIC MEATLOAF

If you thought you couldn't make meatloaf in a slow cooker, you'll be pleasantly surprised. The method I use wraps the meatloaf in an aluminum foil pouch, which is then placed on top of baby potatoes, making a complete meal. The potatoes become fork-tender and can be served as is or easily mashed using a potato masher. For extra flavor, top your meatloaf with your favorite glaze. I like a mixture of ketchup, ground mustard, and Worcestershire sauce.

1½ pounds rainbow potatoes

1½ cups Chicken Stock (page 125)

1½ pounds ground beef, or meatloaf blend

1 teaspoon kosher salt

¼ teaspoon freshly ground black pepper

½ teaspoon onion powder

2 tablespoons Worcestershire sauce

1 cup panko bread crumbs

2 large eggs, beaten

Serves **8**
Prep time: **15 minutes**
Cook time: **8 hours (Low)**
DAIRY-FREE
NUT-FREE

Per Serving (1 slice with 3 ounces potatoes)
Calories: 252; Fat: 6g;
Protein: 23g;
Total Carbohydrates: 26g;
Fiber: 3g; Sugar: 2g;
Sodium: 365mg

1. Put the potatoes in your slow cooker insert. Pour the chicken stock over them.

2. In a large bowl, mix the ground beef, salt, pepper, onion powder, Worcestershire sauce, panko, and eggs to combine.

3. Tear off a piece of aluminum foil large enough to wrap around the meatloaf. Place the meat mixture in the center of the foil. Shape the mixture into an oval loaf that will fit inside the slow cooker insert with the lid closed. Seal the foil around the meatloaf and place it on top of the potatoes. Cover the cooker and cook on Low heat for 8 hours.

4. Carefully discard the fat from inside the foil pack. Serve the meatloaf with the potatoes.

5. Refrigerate any leftovers in an airtight container or freeze for future use (see chart, page 12).

COLLARD GREENS WITH PORK JOWL BACON

Collard greens are as Southern as cheese grits. They're served as part of a traditional New Year's Day meal, but I say they're wonderful any time they're in season. Collards need to be rinsed thoroughly to remove any dirt. You'll want to remove the spines too, as they can be tough. Then, just give the leaves a rough chop and you're set. Don't be concerned that they fill the slow cooker; they cook down substantially.

¾ pound pork jowl bacon, quartered

½ onion, finely chopped

2 tablespoons apple cider vinegar

2 tablespoons packed light brown sugar

1 teaspoon kosher salt, plus more for seasoning

4 cups Chicken Stock (page 125)

2 bunches fresh collards, rinsed, spines removed, leaves roughly chopped

Serves **4 to 6**
Prep time: **15 minutes**
Cook time: **8 hours (Low)**
DAIRY-FREE
NUT-FREE

Tip: Use a 1-pound bag of prepared collard greens to save prep time.

Per Serving (½ cup)
Calories: 663; Fat: 60g;
Protein: 12g;
Total Carbohydrates: 20g;
Fiber: 9g; Sugar: 8g;
Sodium: 353mg

1. In your slow cooker insert, stir together the bacon, onion, vinegar, brown sugar, salt, and chicken stock.

2. Add the collards, pressing the pieces down into the liquid. Cover the cooker and cook on Low heat for 8 hours.

3. Remove and discard the bacon. Taste the collards and add more salt, as needed.

4. Refrigerate any leftovers in an airtight container or freeze for future use (see chart, page 12).

CORNED BEEF AND CABBAGE

Corned beef and cabbage is probably the most traditional St. Patrick's Day meal there is. Of course, you don't have to wait for St. Patrick's Day. Once the corned beef is cooked, you can shred, slice, or shave it, then serve it with a side of cabbage. Be sure to cut the core out of the cabbage before placing it in the slow cooker, because it's too tough to eat.

2 celery stalks, finely chopped

2 carrots, cut into 2-inch sections

1 onion, finely chopped

1½ pounds baby red potatoes

1 (2½-pound) corned beef brisket with

seasoning packet (such as Cattlemen's Ranch brand)

6 cups water

2 bay leaves

Kosher salt

Freshly ground black pepper

½ head cabbage, cored, leaves chopped

Serves **4 to 6**
Prep time: **15 minutes**
Cook time: **8 hours, 15 minutes (Low)**
DAIRY-FREE
NUT-FREE

Tip: The seasoning packet that comes with the brisket includes a variety of pickling spices and can be salty. Check the seasoning at the end of the cooking time before adding more salt, as needed.

Per Serving (3 ounces corned beef, plus cabbage)
Calories: 264; Fat: 10g;
Protein: 14g;
Total Carbohydrates: 31g;
Fiber: 6g; Sugar: 7g;
Sodium: 842mg

1. In your slow cooker insert, combine the celery, carrots, onion, and red potatoes. Place the brisket on top, fat-side up. Sprinkle the seasoning packet on top of the brisket.

2. Pour the water over the brisket and add the bay leaves. Cover the cooker and cook on Low heat for 8 hours.

3. Remove and discard the bay leaves. Taste and add salt and pepper, as needed.

4. Add the cabbage to the cooker, pressing it down into the liquid. Re-cover the cooker and cook for 15 minutes more or until the cabbage is softened.

5. Refrigerate any leftovers in an airtight container or freeze for future use (see chart, page 12).

FRENCH DIP SAMMIES

French dip sandwiches are one of my favorites. There's just something about tender beef and melted cheese, sandwiched between toasted bread, being dipped into sauce. A simple mix of spices is rubbed onto the roast, and into the slow cooker it goes! A generous pouring of stock will end up making the signature dipping sauce. So go ahead and dip it like it's hot.

1 teaspoon kosher salt, plus more for seasoning

½ teaspoon onion powder

½ teaspoon garlic powder

½ teaspoon freshly ground black pepper, plus more for seasoning

1 (2-pound) chuck roast

4 cups Beef Stock (page 123)

6 hoagie rolls, split

6 slices Swiss cheese

Serves **6**
Prep time: **15 minutes**
Cook time: **8 hours (Low)**
NUT-FREE

Tip: Substitute provolone for the Swiss cheese.

Per Serving (1 sandwich)
Calories: 426; Fat: 18g;
Protein: 42g;
Total Carbohydrates: 23g;
Fiber: 1g; Sugar: 3g;
Sodium: 554mg

1. In a small bowl, stir together the salt, onion powder, garlic powder, and pepper.

2. Pat the roast dry with paper towels. Rub the spice mixture all over the roast and place it in your slow cooker insert.

3. Pour the beef stock around the roast, not on top, to avoid washing off the spice rub. Cover the cooker and cook on Low heat for 8 hours. Taste and add more salt and pepper, as needed.

4. Using two forks, shred the roast in the cooker.

5. Preheat the broiler.

6. Place the rolls on a rimmed baking sheet and place 1 cheese slice in each roll. Watching carefully, broil just long enough to melt the cheese, 1 to 2 minutes.

7. Divide the meat among the rolls. Serve with a side of jus, the cooking liquid from the roast.

8. Refrigerate any leftovers in an airtight container or freeze for future use (see chart, page 12).

GINGER-SOY PULLED PORK

This savory pulled pork dish is rich and flavorful from the soy sauce, brown sugar, ginger, and sesame oil. Regular soy sauce contains a lot of sodium, so I like to use a lower-sodium version. This pulled pork can be served over a bed of rice with sliced scallions and a sprinkling of sesame seeds, or even made into a sandwich with a spoonful of coleslaw on top.

1 (2½-pound) pork loin

½ cup low-sodium
soy sauce

½ onion, finely chopped

3 garlic cloves, minced

2 tablespoons honey

2 tablespoons packed
light brown sugar

1 tablespoon ginger paste

1 tablespoon sesame oil

Serves **10**
Prep time: **15 minutes**
Cook time: **8 hours (Low)**
DAIRY-FREE
NUT-FREE

Tips: Ginger paste in a tube can typically be found in the refrigerated section of most grocery stores. Substitute freshly grated ginger for the paste in the same amount.

Per Serving (½ cup)
Calories: 196; Fat: 6g;
Protein: 26g;
Total Carbohydrates: 8g;
Fiber: 0g; Sugar: 6g;
Sodium: 516mg;

1. Put the pork loin in your slow cooker insert. In a medium bowl, stir together the soy sauce, onion, garlic, honey, brown sugar, ginger paste, and sesame oil. Pour the mixture over the pork. Cover the cooker and cook on Low heat for 8 hours.

2. Using two forks, shred the pork in the cooker before serving.

3. Refrigerate any leftovers in an airtight container or freeze for future use (see chart, page 12).

BULGOGI

Bulgogi is a spicy Korean grilled beef dish. This slow cooker take on the popular recipe helps you get all the flavor with none of the fuss. If you're not a big fan of spice, use less sriracha. Serve this beef over cooked rice (jasmine rice works well), and garnish it with a sprinkling of sesame seeds and sliced scallion.

1½ pounds flank steak, cut into strips

2 tablespoons cornstarch

1 cup Beef Stock (page 123)

½ cup low-sodium soy sauce

2 tablespoons sesame oil

2 tablespoons rice wine vinegar

1 tablespoon sriracha

1 tablespoon ginger paste

½ teaspoon garlic powder

½ teaspoon onion powder

Serves **8**
Prep time: **15 minutes**
Cook time: **8 hours (Low)**
DAIRY-FREE
NUT-FREE

Tip: Substitute your favorite hot sauce for the sriracha.

Per Serving (½ cup)
Calories: 166; Fat: 8g;
Protein: 20g;
Total Carbohydrates: 3g;
Fiber: 0g; Sugar: 0g;
Sodium: 619mg

1. In a large zip-top bag, combine the flank steak and cornstarch. Seal the bag and shake to coat the steak. Transfer the steak to your slow cooker insert.

2. In a small bowl, whisk the beef stock, soy sauce, sesame oil, vinegar, sriracha, ginger paste, garlic powder, and onion powder to blend. Pour the sauce over the steak. Cover the cooker and cook on Low heat for 8 hours.

3. Refrigerate any leftovers in an airtight container or freeze for future use (see chart, page 12).

LAMB SHAWARMA

Shawarma is a fabulously fragrant Middle Eastern dish. This rendition includes tender chunks of lamb covered in an array of spices. My favorite way to enjoy lamb shawarma is wrapped in a warm pita, topped with diced tomato, onion slices, and tahini sauce. If you're not feeling like a wrap, serve it over basmati rice.

1 onion, cut into slices

1 pound lamb stew meat

2 tablespoons extra-virgin olive oil

2 teaspoons ground turmeric

2 teaspoons paprika

2 teaspoons ground cumin

2 teaspoons kosher salt, plus more for seasoning

1 teaspoon ground coriander

1 teaspoon ground allspice

½ teaspoon ground cinnamon

½ teaspoon ground ginger

¼ teaspoon ground cloves

⅛ teaspoon cayenne pepper

½ cup Chicken Broth (page 124)

Serves **4**
Prep time: **15 minutes**
Cook time: **8 hours (Low)**
DAIRY-FREE
NUT-FREE

Tip: Measure and mix the spices the night before for convenience when assembling.

Per Serving (1 cup)
Calories: 237; Fat: 13g;
Protein: 23g;
Total Carbohydrates: 5g;
Fiber: 2g; Sugar: 1g;
Sodium: 1241mg

1. Put the onion slices in your slow cooker insert.

2. In a large zip-top bag, combine the lamb, olive oil, turmeric, paprika, cumin, salt, coriander, allspice, cinnamon, ginger, cloves, and cayenne. Seal the bag and massage the meat to coat it in the spices. Transfer the lamb to the slow cooker insert.

3. Add the chicken broth. Cover the cooker and cook on Low heat for 8 hours. Taste and add more salt, as needed.

4. Refrigerate any leftovers in an airtight container or freeze for future use (see chart, page 12).

MARSALA-BRAISED VEAL SHORT RIBS

Marsala isn't just for chicken dishes; this fortified wine from Sicily pairs beautifully with beef as well. Here, veal short ribs are seasoned and then browned to lock in the flavor. The onion and garlic hit the pan to soften, followed by a quick deglaze with the Marsala to absorb every bit of flavor left over from the ribs.

2 pounds veal short ribs

1 teaspoon kosher salt, plus more for seasoning

½ teaspoon freshly ground black pepper, plus more for seasoning

1 tablespoon extra-virgin olive oil

½ onion, finely chopped

3 garlic cloves, minced

1½ cups Marsala wine

1 cup Beef Stock (page 123)

2 thyme sprigs

Serves **4**
Prep time: **15 minutes**
Cook time: **8 hours (Low)**
DAIRY-FREE
NUT-FREE

Tip: Use pre-cut onion and pre-minced garlic for convenience or prepare the vegetables the night before to save time in the morning.

Per Serving (1 rib)
Calories: 568; Fat: 33g;
Protein: 45g;
Total Carbohydrates: 7g;
Fiber: 0g; Sugar: 1g;
Sodium: 464mg

1. Season the ribs with the salt and pepper.

2. In a heavy-bottomed pan over medium heat, heat the olive oil. Add the ribs and cook, turning, until evenly browned on all sides. Transfer to your slow cooker insert.

3. Add the onion and garlic to the hot pan. Sauté until just softened. Stir the Marsala into the pan, scraping up the browned bits from the bottom of the pan. Transfer the mixture to the slow cooker insert.

4. Add the beef stock and thyme. Cover the cooker and cook on Low heat for 8 hours. Serve the ribs either bone-in or shredded.

5. Refrigerate any leftovers in an airtight container or freeze for future use (see chart, page 12).

MEATBALL SUBS

Meatball subs are always a crowd-pleaser. Three large meatballs swimming in sauce sit on a bed of melted provolone cheese and a toasted roll. Pure comfort. Heads up: You're going to need extra napkins for this dish, but after one bite, I'm sure you won't mind.

Nonstick cooking spray

1½ pounds ground beef, or 1 pound ground beef plus 8 ounces meatloaf blend

½ cup panko bread crumbs

½ cup whole milk

1 large egg, beaten

1 teaspoon kosher salt

½ teaspoon garlic powder

½ teaspoon onion powder

3 cups Marinara Sauce (page 130)

6 hoagie rolls, split

6 slices provolone cheese

Serves **6**
Prep time: **15 minutes**
Cook time: **8 hours (Low)**
NUT-FREE

Tips: Substitute traditional bread crumbs for the panko and use your favorite store-bought marinara sauce.

Per Serving (1 roll with 3 meatballs)
Calories: 463; Fat: 18g;
Protein: 40g;
Total Carbohydrates: 38g;
Fiber: 3g; Sugar: 10g;
Sodium: 731mg

1. Coat your slow cooker insert with cooking spray.

2. In a large bowl, mix the ground beef, panko, milk, egg, salt, garlic powder, and onion powder. Using a large cookie scoop, scoop out 18 meatballs. Transfer them to the prepared slow cooker insert, stacking the meatballs if necessary.

3. Pour the marinara sauce over the meatballs, making sure each meatball is covered. Cover the cooker and cook on Low heat for 8 hours.

4. Preheat the broiler.

5. Place the hoagie rolls on a rimmed baking sheet, then place a slice of cheese in each roll. Broil just until the cheese melts, 1 to 2 minutes. Top each bun with 3 meatballs and some sauce.

6. Refrigerate any leftovers in an airtight container or freeze for future use (see chart, page 12).

POMEGRANATE-BRAISED SHORT RIBS

Beef short ribs are such a versatile dish. Depending on the way you serve them, bone-in or shredded, they're not only easy enough for a weeknight meal but they're also elegant enough for entertaining. These ribs are braised in pomegranate juice and red wine to give them a bold flavor. Braising them low and slow yields fall-off-the-bone tender meat. Serve the ribs over mashed potatoes, polenta, or pasta.

2 pounds beef short ribs, cut into individual ribs

1 teaspoon kosher salt, plus more for seasoning

¼ teaspoon freshly ground black pepper, plus more for seasoning

1 tablespoon extra-virgin olive oil

2 cups Beef Stock (page 123)

½ cup pomegranate juice (I like Pom Wonderful brand)

½ cup red wine, such as shiraz

Serves **4**
Prep time: **15 minutes**
Cook time: **8 hours (Low)**
DAIRY-FREE
NUT-FREE

Tips: If you have time, leave the ribs on the counter for 30 minutes to let them come to room temperature before browning. Save the leftover bones to make Beef Stock (page 123) or Beef Broth (page 122).

Per Serving (1 short rib)
Calories: 585; Fat: 43g;
Protein: 40g;
Total Carbohydrates: 5g;
Fiber: 0g; Sugar: 4g;
Sodium: 481mg

1. Season the ribs all over with the salt and pepper.

2. In a heavy-bottomed pan over medium heat, heat the olive oil. Add the ribs and cook, turning, until the ribs are evenly browned on all sides. Transfer the ribs to your slow cooker insert.

3. Add the beef stock, pomegranate juice, and wine. Cover the cooker and cook on Low heat for 8 hours. Taste and add more salt and pepper, as needed.

4. Refrigerate any leftovers in an airtight container or freeze for future use (see chart, page 12).

PORK WITH SAUERKRAUT

Pork, apples, and sauerkraut were made for each other and come together wonderfully in this filling and comforting meal. If you have time, sear the pork loin first to give it even more flavor.

1 (2½-pound) pork loin

1 teaspoon kosher salt

½ teaspoon freshly ground black pepper

1 apple, peeled, cored, and diced (I like Gala or Fuji varieties)

1 onion, finely chopped

24 ounces sauerkraut

4 tablespoons (½ stick) unsalted butter

½ cup water

2 tablespoons apple cider vinegar

Serves **5**
Prep time: **15 minutes**
Cook time: **8 hours (Low)**
NUT-FREE

Tip: Don't drain the liquid from your sauerkraut; you'd be pouring out delicious briny flavor!

Per Serving (8 ounces pork with sauerkraut)
Calories: 436; Fat: 19g;
Protein: 52g;
Total Carbohydrates: 13g;
Fiber: 5g; Sugar: 7g;
Sodium: 1246mg

1. Season the pork all over with the salt and pepper and put it in your slow cooker insert.

2. Add the apple, onion, sauerkraut, butter, water, and vinegar. Mix to combine. Cover the cooker and cook on Low heat for 8 hours. Taste and add more salt and pepper, as needed. Slice the pork and serve it with the sauerkraut.

3. Refrigerate any leftovers in an airtight container or freeze for future use (see chart, page 12).

SLOPPY JOES

I'm not sure who Joe is, but I do love his sandwiches. These loose meat sandwiches are a family favorite, and this recipe makes enough to feed a crowd. I like to toast the buns before serving so they stand up to the messiness of this super-saucy sandwich. Top with dill pickle slices and serve with fries for a complete meal. Don't forget extra napkins!

2 pounds ground beef

1 onion, finely chopped

2 garlic cloves, minced

2 (8-ounce) cans tomato sauce

1 cup ketchup

2 tablespoons packed light brown sugar

2 tablespoons chili powder

1 tablespoon Worcestershire sauce

1 teaspoon kosher salt

1 teaspoon dry mustard

12 hamburger buns

Serves **12**
Prep time: **15 minutes**
Cook time: **8 hours (Low)**
DAIRY-FREE
NUT-FREE

Tip: Prepare the onion and garlic and brown them with the meat the night before, for convenience when assembling.

Per Serving (½ cup)
Calories: 269; Fat: 6g;
Protein: 21g;
Total Carbohydrates: 34g;
Fiber: 2g; Sugar: 12g;
Sodium: 602mg

1. In a large heavy-bottomed pan over medium heat, cook the ground beef, onion, and garlic, stirring to break up the meat with a spoon, until the beef is evenly browned and no longer pink. Drain and discard the excess fat. Transfer the meat mixture to your slow cooker insert.

2. Stir in the tomato sauce, ketchup, brown sugar, chili powder, Worcestershire sauce, salt, and mustard. Cover the cooker and cook on Low heat for 8 hours. Top the buns with the beef mixture to serve.

3. Refrigerate any leftovers in an airtight container or freeze for future use (see chart, page 12).

SPIRAL HAM WITH APRICOT-BOURBON GLAZE

There's just something irresistible about a sweet glaze on a savory ham, and the combination tastes even better when it's an apricot-bourbon glaze. A simple grating of black pepper pulls the sweet flavors together. When the ham is done, be sure to get the glaze pooled in the bottom of the cooker. I find the easiest way to spread the glaze between the ham slices is with a small silicone basting brush. Serve the ham with the classic sides: mashed potatoes and green beans.

Nonstick cooking spray

1 (5- to 6-pound) spiral ham

¼ cup apricot preserves

2 tablespoons bourbon

2 tablespoons Dijon mustard

¼ cup packed light brown sugar

½ teaspoon freshly ground black pepper

Serves **10 to 12**
Prep time: **10 minutes**
Cook time: **8 hours (Low)**
DAIRY-FREE
NUT-FREE

Tip: Before starting, make sure your ham fits in the slow cooker with the lid on.

Per Serving (8 ounces ham)
Calories: 351; Fat: 8g;
Protein: 52g;
Total Carbohydrates: 16g;
Fiber: 0g; Sugar: 15g;
Sodium: 1720mg

1. Coat your slow cooker insert with cooking spray. Place the ham, cut-side down, in the prepared insert.

2. In a small bowl, whisk the preserves, bourbon, Dijon, brown sugar, and pepper to blend. Pour the glaze over the ham. Cover the cooker and cook on Low heat for 8 hours. Spread the glaze from the bottom of the cooker between the slices of ham (see headnote) and serve.

3. Refrigerate any leftovers in an airtight container or freeze for future use (see chart, page 12).

STOUT-BRAISED LAMB SHANKS

Stout-braised lamb shanks are bold and beautiful. The shanks are seasoned with salt and pepper and browned. The vegetables go into the hot pan to soak up the leftover flavor from the shanks and then everything goes into the slow cooker. The sauce this recipe produces after hours of cooking is deep and delicious. Serve as is or puree the sauce with an immersion blender for a silky-smooth consistency. Either way, it's delicious.

4 lamb shanks

1 teaspoon kosher salt, plus more for seasoning

¼ teaspoon freshly ground black pepper, plus more for seasoning

1 tablespoon extra-virgin olive oil

1 onion, finely chopped

2 garlic cloves, minced

2 carrots, finely chopped

2 celery stalks, finely chopped

1 (8-ounce) can tomato sauce

1 (14.9-ounce) can Guinness stout

1 cup Beef Stock (page 123)

Serves **4**
Prep time: **15 minutes**
Cook time: **8 hours (Low)**
DAIRY-FREE
NUT-FREE

Tip: Prepare the vegetables the night before, for convenience.

Per Serving (1 lamb shank)
Calories: 248; Fat: 12g;
Protein: 13g;
Total Carbohydrates: 15g;
Fiber: 3g; Sugar: 5g;
Sodium: 383mg

1. Season the lamb shanks all over with the salt and pepper.

2. In a heavy-bottomed pan over medium heat, heat the olive oil. Add the lamb shanks and cook, turning, until they are evenly browned on all sides. Transfer the shanks to your slow cooker insert.

3. Add the onion, garlic, carrots, and celery to the hot pan. Sauté until just softened. Transfer the vegetables to the slow cooker insert.

4. Stir in the tomato sauce, Guinness, and beef stock. Cover the cooker and cook on Low heat for 8 hours. Taste and add more salt and pepper, as needed.

5. Refrigerate any leftovers in an airtight container or freeze for future use (see chart, page 12).

CLASSIC PULLED PORK

Classic pulled pork is a staple in Southern cuisine and with good reason, because it's ridiculously delicious. It was also made for low and slow cooking. The savory meat begs to be paired with barbecue sauce and turned into a sandwich, butt (see what I did there?) that's not all you can do with it. Pork butt is a great budget-friendly cut that can stretch into multiple meals, any way you like it.

1 (4½-pound) boneless half-butt pork roast

2 tablespoons kosher salt

2 tablespoons packed light brown sugar

1 teaspoon chili powder

1 teaspoon red pepper flakes

1 teaspoon garlic powder

1 (12.5-ounce) can beer

Serves **8 to 10**
Prep time: **10 minutes**
Cook time: **8 hours (Low)**
DAIRY-FREE
NUT-FREE

Tip: Substitute a can of cola, if you prefer not to use beer.

Per Serving (1 cup)
Calories: 371; Fat: 10g;
Protein: 57g;
Total Carbohydrates: 5g;
Fiber: 0g; Sugar: 3g;
Sodium: 1010mg

1. Put the roast on a rimmed baking sheet and pat it dry with a paper towel.

2. In a small bowl, stir together the salt, brown sugar, chili powder, red pepper flakes, and garlic powder. Rub the spice mixture over all sides of the roast. Place the roast in the slow cooker insert.

3. Pour the beer around the roast, not on top, to avoid washing off the spice rub. Cover the cooker and cook on Low heat for 8 hours.

4. Transfer the cooked roast to a clean rimmed baking sheet. Using two forks, shred it and serve.

5. Discard the liquid remaining in the cooker.

6. Refrigerate any leftovers in an airtight container or freeze for future use (see chart, page 12).

VEAL OSSO BUCO

Osso buco is a specialty from the Lombardy region of Italy. What does it mean? Osso buco translates to "bone with hole" which, frankly, sounds better in Italian. Osso buco is made with veal shanks braised in wine and stock for hours until they become fall-off-the-bone tender. Traditionally, osso buco is served over a bed of polenta or risotto with a garnish of gremolata.

2 veal shanks

1 teaspoon kosher salt, plus more for seasoning

½ teaspoon freshly ground black pepper, plus more for seasoning

½ cup all-purpose flour

1 tablespoon extra-virgin olive oil

1 onion, finely chopped

2 carrots, finely chopped

1 celery stalk, finely chopped

2 garlic cloves, minced

½ cup white wine

1½ cups Chicken Stock (page 125)

2 bay leaves

Serves **4**
Prep time: **15 minutes**
Cook time: **8 hours (Low)**
DAIRY-FREE
NUT-FREE

Tip: Prepare the vegetables the night before, for convenience.

Per Serving (½ shank)
Calories: 394; Fat: 12g;
Protein: 46g;
Total Carbohydrates: 19g;
Fiber: 2g; Sugar: 3g;
Sodium: 509mg

1. Season the veal shanks all over with the salt and pepper. Put the flour in a large zip-top bag and add the seasoned shanks. Seal the bag and shake to coat the veal.

2. In a heavy-bottomed pan over medium heat, heat the olive oil. Add the shanks and cook, turning, until they are evenly browned on all sides. Transfer the shanks to your slow cooker insert.

3. Add the onion, carrots, celery, and garlic to the hot pan. Sauté just until softened. Stir the white wine into the pan, scraping up the browned bits from the bottom of the pan to deglaze it. Transfer the vegetables to the slow cooker insert.

4. Add the chicken stock and bay leaves. Cover the cooker and cook on Low heat for 8 hours.

5. Remove and discard the bay leaves. Taste and add more salt and pepper, as needed.

6. Refrigerate any leftovers in an airtight container or freeze for future use (see chart, page 12).

PORK TENDERLOIN WITH POTATOES

This tenderloin is seasoned with a big, bold blend of spices that includes chili pepper, black pepper, paprika, chipotle, onion, garlic, and salt. You can typically find this blend in the spice aisle of your grocery store. The potatoes cook in a bath of chicken stock until fork-tender, after which they can be turned into a quick mash or served whole with a slice of pork.

1½ pounds baby Dutch yellow potatoes

2 cups Chicken Stock (page 125)

1 teaspoon kosher salt

1¾ pounds pork tenderloin, trimmed and halved crosswise

2 tablespoons Southwest seasoning (I like McCormick Gourmet brand)

1 tablespoon extra-virgin olive oil

Serves **6**
Prep time: **15 minutes**
Cook time: **8 hours (Low)**
DAIRY-FREE
NUT-FREE

Tip: Substitute new potatoes for the baby Dutch yellow potatoes.

Per Serving (1 serving pork with 4 ounces potatoes)
Calories: 251; Fat: 5g;
Protein: 30g;
Total Carbohydrates: 20g;
Fiber: 3g; Sugar: 1g;
Sodium: 271mg

1. Put the potatoes in the slow cooker insert. Pour the stock over them and season with the salt.

2. Place the pork on a sheet of aluminum foil large enough to wrap around it. Sprinkle the pork with the seasoning and drizzle it with the olive oil. Rub the spice mixture all over the tenderloin. Wrap and seal the aluminum foil around the pork. Place the tenderloin packet on the potatoes in the slow cooker insert. Cover the cooker and cook on Low heat for 8 hours.

3. Refrigerate any leftovers in an airtight container or freeze for future use (see chart, page 12).

LEG OF LAMB

This elegant, practically effortless meal is perfect for company. Boneless leg of lamb is seasoned with herbes de Provence salt and garlic, then cooked with stock and wine. Herbes de Provence salt is a blend of herbs typically found in the South of France combined with salt for an all-in-one seasoning that pairs beautifully with lamb.

1 (3- to 3½-pound) boneless leg of lamb

3 garlic cloves, halved

2 tablespoons herbes de Provence salt, or herbes de Provence spice blend plus 1 teaspoon kosher salt, plus more for seasoning

¾ pound baby Dutch yellow potatoes

1 cup red wine

5 cups Chicken Stock (page 125)

Serves **6 to 8**
Prep time: **15 minutes**
Cook time: **8 hours (Low)**
DAIRY-FREE
NUT-FREE

Tip: Remove the lamb from the refrigerator 30 minutes before cooking, if possible. This allows for more even cooking.

Per Serving (8 ounces lamb)
Calories: 391; Fat: 13g;
Protein: 47g;
Total Carbohydrates: 11g;
Fiber: 1g; Sugar: 0g;
Sodium: 185mg

1. Use a small sharp knife to cut 6 slits in the lamb, spacing the slits evenly around the roast. Insert the garlic into the slits. Rub the herbes de Provence salt all over the lamb. Put the lamb in your slow cooker insert.

2. Arrange the potatoes around the lamb, then pour the red wine and chicken stock around the lamb. Cover the cooker and cook on Low heat for 8 hours. Taste and add more herbes de Provence salt, as needed.

3. Remove the lamb and let it rest for 15 minutes before slicing and serving with the potatoes.

4. Refrigerate any leftovers in an airtight container or freeze for future use (see chart, page 12).

**NATURALLY SWEET
APPLESAUCE, 132**

HOMEMADE STAPLES

BEEF BROTH

Rich beef broth can be used in soups, stews, sauces, or even just to sip on its own. This recipe yields a hefty 12 cups, but it is easily freezable for future use. I like to store my broth in quart-size mason jars, which don't take up too much room in the refrigerator or freezer. Because everyone's tastes are different, tailor the sodium level to your preference.

2 to 3 pounds beef bones, with some meat still attached

2 carrots, halved

2 celery stalks, halved

1 onion, quartered

2 garlic cloves, crushed

2 bay leaves

1 teaspoon kosher salt

12 cups water

Makes **12 cups**
Prep time: **5 minutes**
Cook time: **8 hours (Low)**
DAIRY-FREE
NUT-FREE

1. In your slow cooker insert, combine the bones, carrots, celery, onion, garlic, bay leaves, salt, and water. Cover the cooker and cook on Low heat for 8 hours.

2. Place a fine-mesh sieve over a large heatproof bowl and strain the broth. Discard the solids.

3. Let cool, then transfer the broth to airtight containers and refrigerate for up to 5 days or freeze for up to 3 months.

Tips: You do not need to peel the carrots or remove the skins from the onion or garlic; they are strained out at the end. Check your local butcher's shop or grocery store butcher for the bones.

Per Serving (1 cup)
Calories: 69; Fat: 4g;
Protein: 6g;
Total Carbohydrates: 1g;
Fiber: 0g; Sugar: 0g;
Sodium: 265mg

BEEF STOCK

The difference between this beef stock and Beef Broth (page 122) is that the broth is made using bones with meat and has salt and other flavorings added. You can use a variety of beef bones to make beef stock, including shanks, ribs, and neck bones. While they cook, they release gelatin that thickens the stock and provides an extra-savory flavor. This recipe yields 12 cups but freezes well for future use.

2 to 3 pounds beef bones
2 celery stalks, halved
2 carrots, halved

1 onion, quartered
12 cups water

Makes **12 cups**
Prep time: **5 minutes**
Cook time: **8 hours (Low)**
DAIRY-FREE
NUT-FREE

1. In your slow cooker insert, combine the bones, celery, carrots, onion, and water. Cover the cooker and cook on Low heat for 8 hours.

2. Place a fine-mesh sieve over a large heatproof bowl and strain the stock. Discard the solids.

3. Let cool, then transfer the stock to airtight containers and refrigerate for up to 5 days or freeze for up to 3 months.

Tip: If you have time, roast the bones before adding them to the slow cooker; roasting helps the bones release their savory flavors. Preheat the oven to 400°F. Place the bones on a sheet pan. Roast for 25 minutes. Turn the bones and roast for 20 minutes more.

Per Serving (1 cup)
Calories: 12; Fat: 0g;
Protein: 2g;
Total Carbohydrates: 1g;
Fiber: 0g; Sugar: 0g;
Sodium: 43mg

CHICKEN BROTH

Homemade chicken broth is rich and versatile. Saving bones from the chicken you use in recipes is always a good idea. Simply collect the bones in a zip-top bag and freeze them as you go until you have enough to make a batch of broth. Waste not, want not. Use chicken broth in soups, stews, and sauces.

About 2 pounds chicken bones (preferably from whole chickens), with some meat attached

2 celery stalks, halved

1 large carrot, halved

1 onion, quartered

4 garlic cloves, smashed

2 bay leaves

1 teaspoon kosher salt

8 cups water

Makes **8 cups**
Prep time: **5 minutes**
Cook time: **8 hours (Low)**
DAIRY-FREE
NUT-FREE

1. In your slow cooker insert, combine the bones, celery, carrot, onion, garlic, bay leaves, salt, and water. Cover the cooker and cook on Low heat for 8 hours.

2. Place a fine-mesh sieve over a large heatproof bowl and strain the broth. Discard the solids.

3. Let cool, then transfer the broth to airtight containers and refrigerate for up to 5 days or freeze for up to 3 months.

Tips: If possible, break the smaller bones before putting them in the slow cooker insert, because that helps release the bone marrow. Also, you do not need to peel the carrot or remove the skins from the onion or garlic; they are strained out at the end.

Per Serving (1 cup)
Calories: 72; Fat: 5g;
Protein: 4g;
Total Carbohydrates: 1g;
Fiber: 0g; Sugar: 0g;
Sodium: 291mg

CHICKEN STOCK

The difference between chicken stock and Chicken Broth (page 124) is that the broth is made using both meat and bones and has salt added. Homemade chicken stock is easy to make and tastier than what you can find at the store. Plus, if you're cooking a whole chicken anyway, why not save the bones and toss them into the slow cooker with a few additional ingredients to reduce waste and "stock up" for future meals.

About 2 pounds chicken bones (preferably from whole chickens)

2 celery stalks, halved

1 large carrot, halved

1 onion, quartered

4 garlic cloves, smashed

2 bay leaves

8 cups water

Makes **8 cups**
Prep time: **5 minutes**
Cook time: **8 hours (Low)**
DAIRY-FREE
NUT-FREE

1. In your slow cooker insert, combine the bones, celery, carrot, onion, garlic, bay leaves, and water. Cover the cooker and cook on Low heat for 8 hours.

2. Place a fine-mesh sieve over a large heatproof bowl and strain the stock. Discard the solids.

3. Let cool, then transfer the stock to airtight containers and refrigerate for up to 5 days or freeze for up to 3 months.

Tip: If possible, break the smaller bones before putting them in the slow cooker insert, because that helps release the bone marrow. Also, you do not need to peel the carrot or remove the skins from the onion or garlic; they are strained out at the end.

Per Serving (1 cup)
Calories: 21; Fat: 1g;
Protein: 2g;
Total Carbohydrates: 1g;
Fiber: 0g; Sugar: 0g;
Sodium: 57mg

CORN BROTH

Corn broth is an excellent vegetarian option and can be used anywhere you would use vegetable broth. Corn broth is especially good to make when sweet corn is in season, although you can also make corn broth from corncobs that have been frozen.

8 corncobs, kernels stripped and reserved for another use (see Tip)

2 celery stalks, halved

1 carrot, halved

1 onion, halved

2 bay leaves

1 teaspoon kosher salt

10 cups water

Makes **10 cups**
Prep time: **15 minutes**
Cook time: **8 hours (Low)**
DAIRY-FREE
NUT-FREE
VEGAN

1. In your slow cooker insert, combine the corncobs, celery, carrot, onion, bay leaves, salt, and water. Cover the cooker and cook on Low heat for 8 hours.

2. Place a fine-mesh sieve over a large heatproof bowl and strain the broth. Discard the solids.

3. Let cool, then transfer the broth to airtight containers and refrigerate for up to 5 days or freeze for up to 3 months.

Tip: Use a tube pan to remove corn kernels from the cobs easily. Stand the cob upright in the center hole of the pan. Holding the cob at the top, carefully cut down the sides to remove the kernels, which are caught in the pan. Save the corn kernels to use in a separate recipe.

Per Serving (1 cup)
Calories: 15; Fat: 0g;
Protein: 0g;
Total Carbohydrates: 3g;
Fiber: 0g; Sugar: 0g;
Sodium: 168mg

VEGETABLE BROTH

Making vegetable broth is a great way to use up vegetable scraps—no need to waste anything. Put leftover bits and pieces from other recipes in a resealable bag or container and refrigerate or freeze until you have enough to make a batch of broth. Vegetable broth, used instead of water, adds flavor to recipes such as rice, soups, stews, and more. The broth freezes well, so keep it on hand for quick and tasty meals whenever.

2 carrots, halved

2 celery stalks, halved

1 onion, quartered

2 bay leaves

1 teaspoon kosher salt

12 cups water

Makes **12 cups**
Prep time: **5 minutes**
Cook time: **8 hours (Low)**
DAIRY-FREE
NUT-FREE
VEGAN

1. In your slow cooker insert, combine the carrots, celery, onion, bay leaves, salt, and water. Cover the cooker and cook on Low heat for 8 hours.

2. Place a fine-mesh sieve over a large heatproof bowl and strain the broth. Discard the solids.

3. Let cool, then transfer the broth to airtight containers and refrigerate for up to 5 days or freeze for up to 3 months.

Tip: For broths like this, there's no need to peel the carrots or remove the onion skin.

Per Serving (1 cup)
Calories: 13; Fat: 0g;
Protein: 0g;
Total Carbohydrates: 3g;
Fiber: 0g; Sugar: 0g;
Sodium: 224mg

BARBECUE SAUCE

Barbecue sauce is a multipurpose condiment here in the South. There are as many different recipes as there are opinions, and every state takes its sauce very seriously. Barbecue sauces are either tomato, mustard, or vinegar based. I love the richness and sweetness of a tomato-based sauce. The obvious pairings for this sauce are chicken, pork, and beef, but it is also great for baked beans, sandwiches, as a dipping sauce, and more.

Nonstick cooking spray

4 cups ketchup

1 cup water

6 ounces pineapple juice

¼ cup packed light brown sugar

3 ounces tomato paste

2 tablespoons unsalted butter

2 tablespoons apple cider vinegar

2 tablespoons Worcestershire sauce

1 teaspoon kosher salt

1 teaspoon smoked paprika

1 teaspoon ground mustard

½ teaspoon garlic powder

½ teaspoon onion powder

Makes **5 cups**
Prep time: **10 minutes**
Cook time: **8 hours (Low)**
NUT-FREE
VEGETARIAN

Tip: Combine the ingredients in an airtight container the night before, then transfer to the slow cooker when ready to cook.

Per Serving (1 cup)
Calories: 364; Fat: 5g;
Protein: 3g;
Total Carbohydrates: 84g;
Fiber: 2g; Sugar: 69g;
Sodium: 2056mg

1. Coat your slow cooker insert with cooking spray.

2. In the slow cooker insert, stir together the ketchup, water, pineapple juice, brown sugar, tomato paste, butter, vinegar, Worcestershire sauce, salt, paprika, ground mustard, garlic powder, and onion powder. Cover the cooker and cook on Low heat for 8 hours.

3. Let cool, then transfer the sauce to airtight containers and refrigerate for up to 5 days or freeze for up to 3 months.

ENCHILADA SAUCE

Enchilada sauce is robust and versatile and can be used to make enchiladas including Cheesy Black Bean and Corn Enchiladas (page 46) and Salsa Chicken Enchiladas (page 70), and one of my favorite soups from this book, Enchilada Soup (page 21). This red enchilada sauce version freezes beautifully, so you'll have some ready for multiple meals.

6 cups tomato sauce

2 cups Vegetable Broth (page 127)

¼ cup chili powder

2 tablespoons ground cumin

1 tablespoon tomato paste

1 tablespoon packed light brown sugar

1 teaspoon onion powder

1 teaspoon garlic powder

½ teaspoon kosher salt

Makes **8 cups**
Prep time: **5 minutes**
Cook time: **8 hours (Low)**
DAIRY-FREE
NUT-FREE
VEGETARIAN

Tip: If you like your sauce on the spicier side, increase the amount of chili powder.

Per Serving (1 cup)
Calories: 72; Fat: 1g;
Protein: 2g;
Total Carbohydrates: 15g;
Fiber: 5g; Sugar: 9g;
Sodium: 1063mg

1. In your slow cooker insert, stir together the tomato sauce, vegetable broth, chili powder, cumin, tomato paste, brown sugar, onion powder, garlic power, and salt. Cover the cooker and cook on Low heat for 8 hours.

2. Let cool, then transfer the sauce to airtight containers and refrigerate for up to 5 days or freeze for up to 3 months.

MARINARA SAUCE

Marinara sauce is a classic Italian tomato sauce made using a combination of tomato products and herbs. Naturally great over spaghetti or on pizza, this sauce is the perfect ingredient shortcut to keep on hand for easy, fast meals. This recipe makes a large batch but it freezes wonderfully, so you can enjoy a delicious meal anytime.

4 (14.5-ounce) cans diced tomatoes

2 (8-ounce) cans tomato sauce

1 (6-ounce) can tomato paste

2 bay leaves

2 teaspoons kosher salt, plus more for seasoning

1 teaspoon red pepper flakes

1 teaspoon dried oregano

1 teaspoon dried basil

½ teaspoon freshly ground black pepper, plus more for seasoning

Makes **8 cups**
Prep time: **10 minutes**
Cook time: **8 hours (Low)**
DAIRY-FREE
NUT-FREE
VEGAN

Tip: If you do not have an immersion blender, use a traditional blender to puree the sauce in batches.

Per Serving (1 cup)
Calories: 64; Fat: 1g;
Protein: 3g;
Total Carbohydrates: 14g;
Fiber: 5g; Sugar: 8g;
Sodium: 663mg

1. In your slow cooker insert, stir together the tomatoes with their juices, tomato sauce, tomato paste, bay leaves, salt, red pepper flakes, oregano, basil, and black pepper. Cover the cooker and cook on Low heat for 8 hours.

2. Remove and discard the bay leaves. Taste and add more salt and pepper, as needed.

3. Using an immersion blender, puree the sauce until it is smooth.

4. Let cool, then transfer the sauce to airtight containers and refrigerate for up to 5 days or freeze for up to 3 months.

MEATY SPAGHETTI SAUCE

A good meaty spaghetti sauce is a great recipe to have in your cooking arsenal. Besides being a classic spaghetti topping, this sauce is incredibly versatile: Try it in lasagna or stuffed shells for a change. Because this recipe has a high yield, it's perfect for use in multiple meals. It also freezes well, so you can space out those scrumptious dinners.

2 tablespoons extra-virgin olive oil

½ onion, finely chopped

2 garlic cloves, minced

1 pound ground beef

2 (14.5-ounce) cans diced tomatoes

1 (15-ounce) can tomato sauce

1 (6-ounce) can tomato paste

1 teaspoon kosher salt, plus more for seasoning

½ teaspoon freshly ground black pepper, plus more for seasoning

1 teaspoon dried basil

1 teaspoon dried oregano

½ cup **Beef Stock (page 123)**

Makes **6 cups**
Prep time: **15 minutes**
Cook time: **8 hours (Low)**
DAIRY-FREE
NUT-FREE

Tip: For a faster morning preparation, complete step 1 the night before.

Per Serving (1 cup)
Calories: 211; Fat: 9g;
Protein: 20g;
Total Carbohydrates: 16g;
Fiber: 5g; Sugar: 10g;
Sodium: 757mg

1. In a heavy-bottomed pan over medium heat, heat the olive oil. Add the onion and garlic. Sauté until softened. Add the beef. Cook, breaking up the meat with a spoon, until it is evenly browned and no longer pink. Drain off any excess fat. Transfer the meat and onion mixture to your slow cooker insert.

2. Stir in the tomatoes with their juices, tomato sauce, tomato paste, salt, pepper, basil, oregano, and beef stock. Cover the cooker and cook on Low heat for 8 hours. Taste and add more salt and pepper, as needed.

3. Let cool, then transfer the sauce to airtight containers and refrigerate for up to 5 days or freeze for up to 3 months.

NATURALLY SWEET APPLESAUCE

Homemade applesauce is incredibly easy to make, and so much more delicious than what you find at the store. This applesauce has no sugar added; it's naturally sweet from the fruit. If you prefer a sweeter sauce, add sugar to taste. I use Gala apples, but use any apple you prefer. No cinnamon sticks? Substitute 1 teaspoon ground cinnamon. I like to store my applesauce in individual mason jars for easy grab-and-go servings.

3 pounds apples, peeled and cored

½ cup water

1 or 2 cinnamon sticks

1 tablespoon freshly squeezed lemon juice

Makes **5 cups**
Prep time: **15 minutes**
Cook time: **8 hours (Low)**
DAIRY-FREE
NUT-FREE
VEGAN

1. In your slow cooker insert, combine the apples, water, cinnamon sticks, and lemon juice. Cover the cooker and cook on Low heat for 8 hours.

2. Remove and discard the cinnamon sticks.

3. Using an immersion blender, puree the applesauce until it reaches your desired consistency. Let cool, then transfer the sauce to airtight containers and refrigerate for up to 3 days.

Tip: If you do not have an immersion blender, use a potato masher or traditional blender to puree the sauce in batches.

Per Serving (½ cup)
Calories: 66; Fat: 0g;
Protein: 0g;
Total Carbohydrates: 17g;
Fiber: 2g; Sugar: 13g;
Sodium: 0mg

DULCE DE LECHE

Dulce de leche translates to "candy of milk" and with just one taste, you'll know why. Surprisingly, to make this recipe you need only one ingredient: sweetened condensed milk. Cooked low and slow in mason jars, the milk becomes beautifully rich and sticky. You'll want to drizzle this on just about everything or give it to your loved ones for a sweet homemade treat.

2 (14-ounce) cans sweetened condensed milk

Makes **3½ cups**
Prep time: **10 minutes**
Cook time: **10 hours (Low)**
NUT-FREE
VEGETARIAN

Per Serving (1 ounce [2 tablespoons])
Calories: 91; Fat: 2g;
Protein: 2g;
Total Carbohydrates: 15g;
Fiber: 0g; Sugar: 15g;
Sodium: 36mg

1. Evenly divide the sweetened condensed milk among 6 (4-ounce) mason jars. Place the lids and rings on the jars, ensuring a tight seal. Transfer the jars to your slow cooker insert. Add enough water to cover the jars completely. Cover the cooker and cook on Low heat for 10 hours.

2. Using tongs, carefully remove the jars from the cooker. Let the jars cool completely before opening or refrigerating them.

3. If refrigerating the jars, remove the jar rings and wipe away any moisture from the lip of the jars before replacing the rings. The jarred dulce de leche will keep in the refrigerator for up to 3 days.

MEASUREMENT CONVERSIONS

	US STANDARD	US STANDARD (OUNCES)	METRIC (APPROXIMATE)
VOLUME EQUIVALENTS (LIQUID)	2 tablespoons	1 fl. oz.	30 mL
	¼ cup	2 fl. oz.	60 mL
	½ cup	4 fl. oz.	120 mL
	1 cup	8 fl. oz.	240 mL
	1½ cups	12 fl. oz.	355 mL
	2 cups or 1 pint	16 fl. oz.	475 mL
	4 cups or 1 quart	32 fl. oz.	1 L
	1 gallon	128 fl. oz.	4 L
VOLUME EQUIVALENTS (DRY)	⅛ teaspoon	——————	0.5 mL
	¼ teaspoon	——————	1 mL
	½ teaspoon	——————	2 mL
	¾ teaspoon	——————	4 mL
	1 teaspoon	——————	5 mL
	1 tablespoon	——————	15 mL
	¼ cup	——————	59 mL
	¼ cup	——————	79 mL
	½ cup	——————	118 mL
	⅔ cup	——————	156 mL
	¾ cup	——————	177 mL
	1 cup	——————	235 mL
	2 cups or 1 pint	——————	475 mL
	3 cups	——————	700 mL
	4 cups or 1 quart	——————	1 L
	½ gallon	——————	2 L
	1 gallon	——————	4 L
WEIGHT EQUIVALENTS	½ ounce	——————	15 g
	1 ounce	——————	30 g
	2 ounces	——————	60 g
	4 ounces	——————	115 g
	8 ounces	——————	225 g
	12 ounces	——————	340 g
	16 ounces or 1 pound	——————	455 g

	FAHRENHEIT (F)	CELSIUS (C) (APPROXIMATE)
OVEN TEMPERATURES	250°F	120°F
	300°F	150°C
	325°F	180°C
	375°F	190°C
	400°F	200°C
	425°F	220°C
	450°F	230°C

RESOURCES

Crock-Pot: Crock-Pot.com

Hamilton Beach: HamiltonBeach.com

Instant Pot: InstantPot.com

Reynolds Kitchens Slow Cooker Liners: ReynoldsKitchens.com

United States Department of Agriculture: USDA.gov

REFERENCES

Jeffers, Mary Katherine. "Cook Slow to Save Time: Four Important Slow
    Cooker Food Safety Tips." United States Department of Agriculture,
    Health and Safety. usda.gov/media/blog/2017/10/24/cook-slow-save
    -time-four-important-slow-cooker-food-safety-tips

United States Department of Agriculture, Food Safety and Inspection
    Service. "Freezing and Food Safety." fsis.usda.gov/wps/portal/fsis/
    topics/food-safety-education/get-answers/food-safety-fact-sheets/
    safe-food-handling/freezing-and-food-safety/CT_Index

United States Department of Agriculture, Food Safety and Inspection
    Service. "Keep Food Safe! Food Safety Basics." fsis.usda.gov/wps/portal
    /fsis/topics/food-safety-education/get-answers/food-safety-fact-sheets
    /safe-food-handling/keep-food-safe-food-safety-basics/ct_index

United States Department of Agriculture, Food Safety and Inspection
    Service. "Slow Cookers and Food Safety." fsis.usda.gov/wps/portal/
    fsis/topics/food-safety-education/get-answers/food-safety-fact-sheets/
    appliances-and-thermometers/slow-cookers-and-food-safety/ct_index

INDEX

ACKNOWLEDGMENTS

To my family, who are the most supportive group of humans on the planet.

You indulge my big crazy dreams and encourage me to keep on keeping on until I reach them. I love y'all to infinity and beyond.

XO

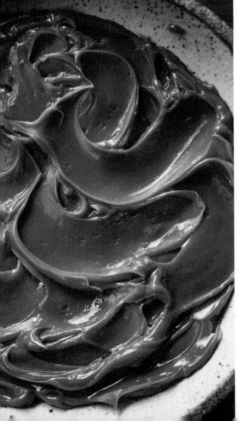

ABOUT THE AUTHOR

Paula Jones is a professional recipe developer, food writer, food photographer, and founder of the popular website *bellalimento.com,* a food blog celebrating simple, seasonal, family-friendly recipes for the past 10 years.

Paula has written and developed recipes for her website as well as for many companies and brands. Her clients include large national brands, public relations firms, and small family-run businesses.

Paula's work has appeared in numerous online publications and in various print media, such as *Southern Living* magazine, and has been nominated for the Saveur Best Food Blog Award. Paula lives in North Carolina.

CPSIA information can be obtained
at www.ICGtesting.com
Printed in the USA
JSHW041654110720
6608JS00006BA/21